The Wisdom
of Humankind

LEO TOLSTOY

The Wisdom of Humankind

TRANSLATED, CONDENSED
AND INTRODUCED BY
Guy de Mallac

CONEXUS PRESS

Publisher's Cataloging in Publication
(Provided by Quality Books, Inc.)

Tolstoy, Leo, graf, 1828-1910.
  The wisdom of humankind / Leo Tolstoy ;
translated, condensed and introduced by Guy de Mallac.
    p. cm.
    Includes bibliographical references.
    ISBN: 0-9637897-4-0

    1. Conduct of life--Quotations, maxims, etc.
  I. Mallac, Guy de, 1936-   II. Title.

BJ1581.2.T64 1999   170'.44
                                QBI98-990013

To order additional copies, contact:
CoNexus Press
6264 Grand River Dr. NE
Ada, MI 49301 USA
tel. 616-682-9022 / fax. 616-682-9023 / conexus@iserv.net
US $13.95 plus $3.00 S&H. Visa & MC accepted.
Trade distributor: APG, Nashville, TN, USA
tel. 800-327-5113 / fax: 800-510-3650

Contents

The Wisdom of Humankind

INTRODUCTORY

1. FAITH, OR RIGHT UNDERSTANDING

In order for us to live our life well, we must know what we should and should not do. To know this, we must understand what we are and the nature of the world in which we live. This has been taught by the wisest and best people of all nations at all times. These teachings agree with each other and they agree with what every person is told by reason and conscience.

TEACHINGS

2. THE SPIRIT WITHIN

In addition to what we see, hear, feel, and learn from people, there is a reality that we do not see, hear, or feel, and about which no one has ever told us anything, but which we know better than anything else in the world. It is that about which we say "I."

3. THERE IS ONE SPIRIT IN ALL

That invisible principle which gives us life we recognize as well in all living beings and we recognize it especially in beings similar to humans.

FAULTS

*Faults or bodily cravings are moral weaknesses
which hinder our oneness with others.*

TEMPTATIONS

False notions (that draw us to faults) about what is good and about our relationships to one another.

SUPERSTITIONS

False doctrines or beliefs used to justify faults and temptations.

POSITIVE APPROACHES AND PRACTICES

*Actions to fight against faults, temptations, and superstitions
and avail ourselves of good.*

CONCLUSION

Efforts to practice self-denial, to be humble, and to be truthful, destroy a person's inner obstacles to the oneness of the soul through love with other beings and with God. Such efforts provide us with the good that is always accessible. Therefore, the things that appear evil to us are only an indication that we have a false understanding of our lives and we are not doing what our own natural good makes possible for us. To that extent, evil is unreal.

Death in terms of the body is not death of the spirit. That which appears to be death is death only for those who see their lives in temporal (material) terms. For those who see life for what it really is—the efforts made to free ourselves of everything that hinders union with God and with others—there is not and cannot be any death.

We have not been told, nor do we need to be told, how the soul will be conscious of itself after the death of the body. For a person who understands life as the ever increasing union of the soul through love with all that is alive, there can be no worry about what will happen to the soul after the body's death.

We see our life as a blessing, if we view it as the constant, ever increasing union of our souls with all living beings and with God. If we try to achieve such union, our life can be nothing other than totally good.

APPENDICES by Guy de Mallac

Acknowledgments

Since I started work at a slow pace in 1981 on what ultimately was to become this edition of *The Wisdom of Humankind*, several individuals helped in various ways: Professor Victor Terras, Professor George Gibian, Professor Gary Jahn, Professor Michael Green, Dr. Ronald Walter, Dr. Arlene Dorius, Lynette Horn, Joel Beversluis, Arthur B. Burton, Glen Woodmansee, and Janice Gale; and a number of students, former students, and other friends. Very resourcefully, Angela Yang, a librarian at the University of California, Irvine, led a team including John Rice, Raj Barot, and Erik Rhode, that helped locate hard-to-find information pertaining to Tolstoy's sources. May I also express my gratitude to Marge Gayatri Devi Ranney, whose warm support has facilitated this project.

Anna Light deserves unique mention here. At intervals from the Fall of 1992 until the Fall of 1993, she generously gave of her time and energy to this project. She did a crucial part of the review of the text, in order for us to edit the thirty-one chapters more accurately. Her participation in major editing facilitated much earlier completion of Tolstoy's thirty-one chapters than would otherwise have been the case. Her contribution to the task has been essential.

Guy de Mallac
December 18, 1998

Introduction

Putting the best expressions of human wisdom between the covers of a single book would be, one might think, a vitally important undertaking. Yet there have been very few attempts at it in our century—for only a dedicated intellectual and spiritual genius of Tolstoy's stature would be equal to the task, and such geniuses are scarce.

The gathering together of the wisdom of humankind was precisely the endeavor for which Tolstoy felt a profound need. This endeavor became the main project of the last seven years of his life (1903–1910). During most of that period, drafts of this work were on his desk, written and rewritten as he devoted most of his thought and energy to the project. The book went through four versions, and from one version to the next Tolstoy improved and refined both content and format. Even on his deathbed he was busy correcting page proofs of the fourth edition.

The final result—the fourth edition—was a creative synthesis, published in Russian shortly after Tolstoy's death, under the title *The Way of Life* (1911). Tolstoy's book is composed of direct quotations from the works of great sages, of paraphrases of similarly important observations, and of passages elucidating Tolstoy's views. All of these entries are merged with one another, and arranged in thirty-one chapters.

Tolstoy's work in gathering the essential wisdom of various cultures and ages has long been known to individual scholars, but not to the broader public. The purpose of the present edition is to fill this awareness gap and to make Tolstoy's comprehensive and insightful work accessible, in compact form, to the general reader. This new edition in English, while based on the authoritative Russian scholarly edition of 1956, is a distillation of Tolstoy's work in the kind of compact edition that the writer himself stated would be desirable. At the time of his death he was in fact planning to bring out such a shorter version of his original work.

Tolstoy's creative summation of the wisdom of the ages was not the only such volume written in this century. Aldous Huxley's *The Perennial Philosophy* (1944) shared some of the aims of Tolstoy's compendium. Both writers focused on ethical values and aimed at conveying morally founded wisdom. In Tolstoy's original work quotations are included from sages ranging from Plato, Marcus Aurelius, and Voltaire to Thoreau and Henry George—all of whom had spoken to the highest common factor of ethically grounded wisdom.

Further, Tolstoy's book is a masterful synthesis of ethical principles rather than a general compilation of however cogent quotations. In the present edition, a condensation and synthesis of Tolstoy's full edition, quotations from other seminal thinkers have been blended with the main statements that comprise Tolstoy's argument in each chapter. Such blending of quotations into a single text seemed suitable for this compact edition.

The Wisdom of Humankind was Tolstoy's last major work. During his last twenty-odd years, he assiduously absorbed and collated the essential philosophical and spiritual experience of humankind in order to produce his powerful creative synthesis.

In this work he embodied an ideal toward which he had

long been striving—the fusion of his discourse with that of the New Testament and other spiritual texts. His aim was to emulate the directness, simplicity, and compelling force of Scripture in order to achieve the striking effectiveness of scriptural discourse. He felt that this high aim was an appropriate one in a book which was to be a summation of the world's wisdom.

As the reader will discover, Tolstoy's writing can appear to some as morally severe. Occasionally, Tolstoy's stance has a sharp-edged, jagged quality (often related to the exacting nature of the perennial wisdom). His search for the broad brush of truthful statement did not permit a gentle gloss or include palliating qualifications. Some generalizations as to desirable and undesirable conduct could use modifications and exceptions. Thus, readers of this work will take from such a rich collation of observations those which are pertinent to their own reasoning or expansive of their own perspectives.

This condensation of Tolstoy's last book is not just one among his important works. Rather, it occupies a unique place among his major works since it is the ultimate expression of Tolstoy's insights. In his own view, this book was the summation of a lifetime of thought and reflection. *The Wisdom of Humankind* may rightly be viewed as Tolstoy's last will and testament. He himself viewed it as such.

This book is intensely contemporary; its perennial message addresses any number of today's key issues. Tolstoy's imprint on several prominent writers, including Matthew Arnold, William Dean Howells, D. H. Lawrence, and Hemingway, was decisive. Similarly, Tolstoy's views influenced the young M. K. Gandhi, and later, through Gandhi's example and writings, had an important impact on Martin Luther King Jr., as well as on countless followers of both of these men. Most of Tolstoy's positions and observations are translatable to contemporary society's concerns with the need for moral responsibility, accountability, and discipline.

The Wisdom of Humankind is, then, a unique and compelling statement of Tolstoy's fundamental message and is his richest gift to us.

The Life of Leo Tolstoy

1828-1910

L eo (Lev) Nikolaevich Tolstoy was born in August 1828
to a well-to-do aristocratic family. He grew up on the
family estate, Yasnaya Polyana (Bright Glade), in the Province of Tula, about 150 miles East of Moscow. When the
child was two, his mother died, and his father when he was
nine. Tolstoy was brought up by an affectionate aunt who
always remained very close to him. At the age of sixteen he
started studying Oriental languages at the University of
Kazan (1844-1847), after which he was briefly engaged in law
studies at the University of St. Petersburg (1849). Disappointed by what these academic institutions had to offer and
the limited intellectual inspiration he received from them, the
young man did not complete a degree in either field. He then
started leading a rather aimless and dissolute life in Moscow
and St. Petersburg.

In 1851, he signed up as a volunteer and followed his
brother into army service in the Caucasus, and in 1852 he
joined the army. He participated in the Crimean war, which
Russia was waging against England, France and Turkey, and
took part in the defense of Sevastopol. A description of
these military experiences was recorded in his volume *The
Sevastopol Sketches,* first serialized in the influential journal *The
Contemporary.* This account attracted considerable attention

for its unvarnished picture of war; in fact, in that early work Tolstoy was already debunking the mystique of military life.

Also written in the early 1850s was Tolstoy's first published work, *Childhood*, a semi-autobiographical narrative about the growing up of a protagonist whom Tolstoy calls Nicholas Irtenev. This was the first part of a trilogy that also included *Boyhood* (1854) and *Youth* (1857). In that early work is presented Tolstoy's notion, which he was to develop later, that conventional education and the pressures of society distort our inborn sense of the meaning of life.

Tolstoy left army service in 1856 and for several years divided his time between his estate, Yasnaya Polyana, and life in St. Petersburg. In 1847 he had started to keep a diary, in which over the ensuing years he recorded an intense dissatisfaction with his libertine existence, listing both his concern with moral improvement and his lapses—drinking, gambling, and dissoluteness. Although during that period Tolstoy developed an interest in farming, his literary activities occupied more and more time. By the late 1850s, his fame as a fiction-writer had grown considerably. This fame was based on such works as: *The Sevastopol Sketches; Two Hussars* and *The Landowner's Morning* (1856); *Youth* (1857); "Three Deaths" and *Family Happiness* (1859); followed by *The Cossacks* in 1863. During that period Tolstoy resisted pressure to reflect in his work overt social concerns and dealt instead with timeless issues: love and marriage, youth, age and death.

During this same time, Tolstoy sporadically attempted to aid and educate the serfs on his estate. There he set up a school for peasant children, stressing a spontaneous approach to learning and the need for children to learn from their natural environment. In 1860 he went on a tour of Western Europe to study educational theories and establishments. The outcome of his investigations and educational experiments is presented in the journal *Yasnaya Polyana*, which he began in 1862.

In September 1862, when he was thirty-four, he married a well-educated aristocrat, Sophia Andreevna Behrs, who was then eighteen. The couple immediately settled on Tolstoy's estate and led a relatively uneventful life, punctuated by occasional visits by relatives and infrequent stays in Moscow. Sophia Behrs bore thirteen children, nine of whom survived. She was a devoted wife who, in addition to looking after the upbringing of her children, copied long-hand his manuscripts (thus copying the whole of *War and Peace* five times). She generally provided Tolstoy with the best conditions for his literary activity. The first decade of their marriage was marked by peacefulness and harmony, which heightened Tolstoy's creativity.

His great achievement of the 1860s was *War and Peace*, usually reckoned among a small handful of the world's most remarkable novels. That novel, written from 1863 to 1867, was first serialized and then published in several volumes in the late 1860s.

This work was received enthusiastically in Russia. As a result of its publication, Tolstoy became Russia's foremost writer. *War and Peace* was soon translated into the world's major languages, spreading the author's fame to many countries. It depicts the fates of three Russian aristocratic families before, during, and after the Napoleonic campaign in Russia in 1812. Chapters on the domestic life of these families alternate with portrayals of military events and how they affect the lives of these and other Russians. Over 600 characters are portrayed in the novel, the majority of them from aristocratic and military milieus.

In the aftermath of the publication of *War and Peace*, Tolstoy underwent much soul-searching and anxiety. These periodic spells of self-probing enabled him to come up with profound insights into the human condition. Some of the intellectual pursuits he then took up were the study of Greek, which allowed him direct contact with the original text of the New Testament, the study of Hebrew, which he applied to the reading of the Jewish *Torah* (the Christian Old Testament), as well as an investigation of various philosophical and scientific domains. By the end of his life, the library at Yasnaya Polyana, which in his father's time had numbered two thousand volumes, counted about 32,000 titles. He drew upon these resources over a period of many decades, which accounts for the breadth and depth of his encyclopedic learning.

Tolstoy's next major achievement was the novel *Anna Karenina*, which he wrote between 1873 and 1876. It was first serialized and then came out as a separate volume.

Along with *War and Peace*, this novel had the greatest impact on the Russian and world public in establishing Tolstoy's reputation as one of the foremost novelists in the world. *Anna Karenina* portrays the fates of two protagonists, Anna Karenina and Levin, and of their respective marriages. Levin (modeled in many respects after Tolstoy) achieves fulfillment in this domestic life and in his self-appointed mission to be a committed landowner, fostering the social and economic well-being of his peasants. Anna Karenina yields to the enticement of her extramarital passion for Vronsky, sacrificing to it her ties with her husband and young son. In so doing, she flaunts the rules society then prescribed for someone of her social status; her life takes a tragic turn, and ends in suicide. In contrast, Levin finds fulfillment in married life and social commitment.

During the writing of *Anna Karenina*, Tolstoy probed deeply into the values in his life, and questioned the motivations for his existence. This had been preceded by an episode in 1869 when Tolstoy went through considerable anxiety and terror; while spending a night in the small town of Arzamas, he perceived, very graphically in his mind and in his flesh, a strong feeling of the inevitability of death. After completion of *Anna Karenina,* renewed acute anxiety brought him to the far-reaching spiritual crisis that he experienced in the late 1870s.

Tolstoy seemed to be provided with everything one could desire: comfortable means, a devoted wife and family, and considerable fame as a writer. Yet he was probing so deeply into the meaning of life that material satisfactions and natural affections did not provide the significance he was searching for. In his spiritual autobiography, *My Confession,* he depicted the development of this search, leading to a crisis. His existential despair grew to the extent that he was contemplating suicide.

Tolstoy found the solution to this crisis—as portrayed in his deeply moving *Confession*—after considering the lives of the Russian peasants on and around his estate. Although they were poor and led a harsh life, sometimes without enough food and with very inadequate housing, they faced life in a cheerful and positive way, with fortitude, and in a constructive spirit. He concluded that existential malaise was a disease peculiar to the idle aristocracy. He realized that the peasants were endowed with a deep belief in life, and decided to emulate that attitude.

From then on Tolstoy simplified his life more and more within the context of a philosophy that included the practice of physical, manual labor. In many respects, he adopted a peasants' way of life. (Various aspects of this world-view, which Tolstoy espoused in the 1880s and developed in the 1890s and 1900s, are presented in "Tolstoy's Search for Wisdom," on page 179.)

During the last decades of his life, Tolstoy's multiple statements and pronouncements illustrating the philosophy he had developed, as well as the personal example he was giving in leading a life of simplicity, attracted numerous visitors to Yasnaya Polyana. The writings propounding his doctrine or philosophy received considerable attention in several countries of Europe, as well in Canada and the United States where committees, groups, or colonies formed with the purpose of implementing his principles. Some of these groups stressed his philosophical and religious views, some his humanitarian notions, while some emphasized communitarian living, the simple life, or sound agricultural practices. Their diversity of philosophical hues and shades illustrated the richness of Tolstoy's inspiration.

Anticipating the notion fostered by his follower Mahatma Gandhi that "property is violence," Tolstoy felt increasingly uneasy about the trappings of well-to-do life around his estate (however much he had simplified his personal life). In the 1880s he had deeded the estate to his wife, but his continuing qualms about what he viewed as the relative luxury of their existence and the retaining of significant means and property triggered Countess Tolstoy's bitter opposition. The last few years of his life were marred by growing estrangement between them.

In late October 1910, accompanied by his daughter Alexandra (his close support and helper), he left Yasnaya Polyana with scanty belongings and no specific destination, intending to lead the life of a simple pilgrim or itinerant. Having caught pneumonia, however, he died at the railway station-master's house in Astapovo, a small railway junction, on November 7, 1910. His death was marked by national mourning in which even the government participated. He was buried in Yasnaya Polyana.

*The Wisdom
of Humankind*

INTRODUCTORY

CHAPTER ONE

Faith, or Right Understanding

Faith is the strength of life.
from *A Confession*

In order to live right, we must know what we ought to do, and what we ought not to do. In order to know this, we need faith, or right understanding. True faith is different from belief in the sense of "blind belief." Faith is the knowledge of what we are, and for what purpose we live in the world. Such is the faith which has been and is held by all who use their reason and understanding.

1. What is true faith, or right understanding?

In order to live right, it is necessary to understand what life is, and how to live it. This one doctrine (teaching) common to all people is true faith. Faith alone can tell us what is this world, which has no limit, and how we must live in this infinite world. If you doubt your faith, it is no longer faith. Faith is only true faith when you have no thought that what you believe could be untrue. There are many and varied beliefs in a person or a people, but there is one faith in God, and that faith is the same for all people.

2. The doctrine (teaching) of true faith is always clear and simple.

True faith shows us what we are and what we ought to do, but it does not tell us what the outcome will be if we do what our faith commands. The doctrine of true faith is so simple and clear that we cannot excuse our evil life by pleading ignorance of the teaching. The law of life asks nothing of us but to love our neighbor. Knowing the true faith is like lighting a lamp in a dark room. All things become clear, and joy enters the soul.

3. True faith is to love God and your neighbor.

Jesus did not say: "You are my disciples if you believe this or that," but, "You are my disciples if you love one another." Faith may differ with different people, and in different times, but love is one and the same at all times and with all people. The true faith is one—to love all that is living. The eternal, the unseen dwells within us right now, in this life. We attain eternal life when we become one with God through our love.

4. Faith guides a person's life.

True faith is knowing what you ought to do and what you

ought not to do in this life. If one person, or even an entire nation, does not live happily, it is only because that person or nation has lost faith. The more clearly we understand the true law of life, the better is our life. In order to escape from the life of misery which they lead, people are in need of one thing alone: they need a faith by which to live, as opposed to their present each-for-himself life. They need a common life, all acknowledging one law and one purpose. To give up this life for life everlasting is impossible, because everlasting life is already in this life.

5. False faith.

The law of life—to love God and your neighbor—is simple and clear. Everyone on attaining reason recognizes it. False teachings keep us from adhering to it and the Kingdom of Heaven from reigning upon earth. The departure from the law of life because of false teachings has made this life harder to bear and more unhappy. Therefore we must not believe any teachings that do not agree with love of God and of neighbor. A special group of people (theologians and clergy) claim that every word of scripture was inspired and written by God. This is untrue: all books are the work of human hands and contain something true and something false. Besides, God's law is revealed equally to *all*, not just to some people.

Do not believe that a faith is true because it is ancient. And do not be disturbed if your faith is not the same as that of your ancestors. We must establish a faith in which we can believe as firmly as our fathers and mothers believed in theirs. To know the true faith, first give up that one in which you blindly believe, and then examine in the light of your reason all you have learned since childhood. Regarding God and his law, listen to the voice of the spirit within you, not to the voice of strangers. It is bad not to know God, but it is worse to acknowledge as God that which is not God.

6. External worship.

True faith is the belief in that one law which is suitable to all the people in the world. It enters the heart in stillness and solitude. True faith consists in always living a decent life, in loving all humanity, and doing unto others as you would have others do unto you. We cannot please God, or deceive him, with formal prayers or rituals; we only deceive ourselves. God does not need the pleas of others on your behalf, nor your gifts, nor your praises regarding things you cannot know. All God requires of us is good works, in the same fashion as a master requires nothing of a laborer but labor. This is the entire law of God.

7. The idea of a reward for a good life is foreign to true faith.

Do not follow a religion because you expect all sorts of future external rewards. True faith yields its blessings only in the present, not in the future. Some teachers try to trick people into good living by terrifying them with threats of punishment and deceiving them with promises of rewards in another world which no one has ever seen. If you serve God for the promise of future bliss, you do not serve God, but your own ends. In false faith a person desires to be rewarded by God for sacrifices. In true faith a person seeks one thing alone: to learn how to please God. Love dwells in the spirit (soul), and whoever unites with it, is happy.

8. Reason verifies the principles of faith.

Reason must be purified and applied in order that we may examine what is taught us by religious teachers. It is not by reason that we attain faith, but reason is necessary to examine faith. Stories about miracles cannot confirm truth; they are not trustworthy. Do not fear to eliminate from your faith all that is unnecessary, physical, visible, and also what is lacking in clearness; the better you purify your faith, the more clearly you will grasp the true law of life. A non-believer is not one who does not believe all that people around him believe, but he is truly a non-believer who thinks he believes something which he really does not believe.

9. The religious consciousness of people is constantly perfecting itself.

While benefiting from the teachings of the wise, we must examine such teachings in the light of our own reason, accepting all that is in agreement with reason. If, in order not to stray from the law of God, you refuse to leave your adopted faith, you are like a traveler who has bound himself with a rope to a post so as not to lose his way. Some of the most ancient religious teachings are no longer suited to our time. Do not forget that if God revealed the truth to the ancients, he still remains the same and can also reveal it to those who live today.

Jesus is a great teacher who preached the true universal religion of love toward God and humans. But it is wrong to think that God has not provided similarly great teachers, or even greater ones. If we think that, after Jesus, God no longer reveals himself directly to people, then when new teachers appear, the same will happen to them as happened to Jesus: people will kill the living prophet in order to make the dead prophet into a God. If Jesus had not departed from the teaching that in his day was considered the truth, we would not have had him as a great teacher. If he had said like the others, "No one can interpret God's law better than

Moses," he would have been nothing and the spirit of God would have departed from him. Today God is as ready to reveal the truth to all those who wish to serve him through their lives.

When rainwater flows from the roof-gutter, it seems to us that the rain came from the roof-gutter. But rain falls from above. Hence, we think that the teachings of the wise come from them, when they come from God. Truth is revealed always and everywhere to those who listen.

TEACHINGS

CHAPTER TWO

The Spirit Within

. . . this real divine self
which lives in every person.
from *Resurrection*

There is something within us which we can neither touch nor see. This something is not the body, but is separated from all else by the body. This is that of which we are conscious as self. It is called the spirit within us or the soul.

1. What is the spirit within?

A person's self (or "I"), regardless of age, remains the same, and this we call the soul. We only know the physical universe through our senses, and therefore cannot know it fully. Only one thing we can truly and fully know, namely our soul.

2. The "I" is spiritual.

Our "I" is not our body, and we cannot define our "I", yet we know it better than anything else; without it, we could know nothing, and we would not be. It is more difficult to understand what my body is than what my soul is. As close as it is to me, the body is something foreign; the soul is really *mine*, the body is not. If we are not conscious of the spirit within us, we merely have not yet learned to be aware of it. Before we know the world, we must first know what is within us. Humans cannot live without a spiritual life. The spirit dwells in everyone, but not all are aware of it.

3. The spirit within and the material world.

We have measured, penetrated, and explored the world and discovered and measured the stars; we continually have new inventions. We have no limit to what we can do, but we lack knowing ourselves; we are like babes. The world, the universe, is too large to be grasped; what we can and must understand is our soul. The soul has always been, it is now and it will never be lost. Humans are nothing compared to the earth, which is nothing compared to the sun and other stars, nor compared to the millions who have lived and will live. Yet, we have within us an idea of ourselves and the universe; this idea is more important than the entire universe, for without this idea within us the universe would not exist.

4. The spiritual and material principles in the human being.

Each of us is an individual, yet within each is a spiritual being, which is the same in all of us. One spiritual being is in us all. There is no body without food, but food is not the body; similarly, without the body there would be no soul, but the soul is not the body. The principle of life is not in the body, but in the soul; the spiritual life is the real life. The soul within us raises us above this life and makes us free and fearless.

5. Conscience is the voice of the spirit within.

In each person dwell two parts (beings), one blind and of the body, the other, seeing and spiritual. The spiritual part of a person is the conscience; when we stray from the right, it tells us. It is the voice of the spiritual being that dwells in all of us. Conscience, as the consciousness of the spiritual being that dwells in all people, is the true guide of human life. Usually what most people call conscience is not the recognition of that spiritual being, but the recognition of what they consider good or evil. The passions may roar loudly, but they subside before the voice of conscience, which is the voice of the Eternal, the Spirit in the human being. The law of goodness is in your own spirit; do not seek it outside, but within.

6. The divine nature of the soul.

The first consciousness that awakes within us is that of being apart from all other material things, or the consciousness of the body. Then we are conscious of that which is separated, or the spirit within. Finally we are conscious of that from which the spirit is separated, the consciousness of All—of God. That part of us which is conscious of that separation is the one spiritual being that dwells in everyone. God is not comprehended by reason (with the mind), but by conscious-ness of him within us. The greatest joy we may know is the joy of realizing the existence within us of a free, rational, loving, and therefore happy being, in other words the con-sciousness of God within us. Do not think: it is I that live. It is not I that live, but that spiritual being that dwells within. I am only the opening through which this being appears. I know God not when I believe what is said about him, but when I am as conscious of him as I am of my own soul. It is as though we always heard a voice behind us, but had no power to turn our heads and see who spoke. This voice speaks in all languages and guides all people, but no one has ever discovered who speaks. If only we obeyed this voice to the letter and accepted it so as not to keep ourselves apart from it even in thought, we would feel that we are one with this voice. The more we consider this voice as our own self, the better our life will be. This voice will open up to us a life of blessedness, because this voice is the voice of God within us. God desires good to all, therefore if we desire good to all (if we love), God lives within us. To forget God is to forget who lives within us and by whom we live. As we need God, so God needs us. You can escape from the most difficult situation the moment you realize that you live not in your body, but in your spirit, and remember that God within you is more powerful than anything in the world. If we ask ourselves "What is that within me that is conscious of what I am doing, thinking, or feeling?" our only answer can be that it is the consciousness of self. This consciousness of self is what we call the spirit.

The fish in a river heard that fish could only live in water, so they began to ask, "What is water?" Finally a very wise old fish answered: "Water is that wherein and whereby we live. The reason you do not know water is that you live in it and

en so, it seems to people at times that they do not
at is God and yet they live in him.

7. True life is not in the body but in the soul, not in the body and in the soul, but in the soul alone.

We must lift up the spirit within us above the body. The body and what is for the body will end, so we should build our life on what will not perish, that is, on the spirit within us. Do what your body asks: seek after glory, honors, and wealth, and your life will be hell. Do what the spirit within you asks: seek after lowliness, mercy, and love, and you will not need any paradise. Paradise will be in your soul. If you live for your soul, you will know what to do, namely the good which the soul demands. When you feel the rise of passions, whims, fears, or hatred, remember that you are not the body, but the soul, and that which upsets you will at once subside.

8. Spiritual blessedness is the only true blessedness.

One who lives by the spirit is free, even if in chains or in prison. The body, reaching fullness, begins to grow feeble, but the life of the spirit constantly develops and gathers strength. If I live for my soul, my happiness gathers strength every day, and I will not fear death; I will need no knowledge of where I am going, but will experience perfect blessedness. If we are aware of the spirit as the basis of our life, we know that we are beyond all danger. An immortal soul requires an immortal task—endless striving after perfection of self and the world.

CHAPTER THREE

There is One Spirit in All

. . . all one's life, all one's soul
which belongs to God,
[some people] give to Caesar . . .
from "Nikolai Palkin"

All living creatures are separated one from another by their bodies, but that which gives them life is one and the same in all of them—the spirit or soul.

1. The consciousness that the soul is godlike unites all humans.

It is not just the same kind of soul, but the same soul (spirit) which lives in all of us, making us all brothers and sisters. We are separated by our bodies, but joined through the same spirit which gives life to everyone. We associate with people, but how do we unite with everyone? Suppose we unite with friends and relatives: what about people we do not know of other nationalities and religions? There are so many people and they differ so much. What are we to do? The only remedy is, without focusing on the diversity among people, to strive to be one with the spirit that dwells within all of us. When I think about all the people everywhere whom I do not know and who know nothing about me, I wonder, is there no tie that binds us together? Somehow I feel, I know that there is a tie between myself and all people in the world, living and dead. I cannot understand it or explain it, but I know it exists.

In everyone there is much that is very good and humane, and also much that is evil and full of hatred. Even suffering brings about different reactions in different people, and sometimes in the same person. Sometimes I regard all creatures with genuine compassion, and brotherly/sisterly feelings, sometimes with the most thorough indifference, and occasionally with a cruel heart that rejoices over their sufferings. This clearly shows that there are within me two different and directly opposite ways to know all human beings:

a) When I know myself as an individual physical body, I feel separated from all others and they seem completely different from me; then I feel nothing toward them but indifference, envy, and hatred.

b) When I know myself as a spiritual being, I feel linked with all other beings, and then I feel love toward them, and sympathy and oneness with them.

The first way separates us with a solid wall, the second way removes the wall and we are joined as one.

If you live for the body you are alone among strangers; if you live for the spirit, all the world is your kin. When entering into conversation with others, if we look searchingly into their eyes, we feel that we are akin to them. Regardless of their station in the world, all humans must be treated alike, with care and respect. Only he is awake and truly lives, who sees himself and God in his neighbor.

2. One and the same spirit lives not only in all humans, but in all living creatures.

The universal spiritual principle that is present in all humans is also present in animals and plants. This was perceived by the Buddha when he said, "All that is living fears pain, all that is living fears death: recognize yourself not only in other humans, but in every living creature; do not kill, do not cause suffering and death. All that is living desires the same things as you: recognize yourself in every living creature."

We human beings are higher than animals, not because we can torture them, but because we are capable of having compassion for them. Compassion for every living thing is most essential to any person who wishes to achieve inner growth. Such compassion toward living creatures is natural to all humans, but it is possible to lose it by degrees; this process occurs in hunters, who grow accustomed to torturing and killing animals without noticing their own cruelty. "You shall not kill!" is a commandment which we should apply not only to humans, but to all living creatures.

Just as we now marvel that once people ate human flesh, so posterity will one day marvel that we, their forefathers, daily killed millions of animals although we could satisfy our hunger both wholesomely and pleasantly with the fruits of the earth and without killing. While realistically we should acknowledge that we cannot live without destroying life to some extent, we can learn to become more and more compassionate.

3. The better our life, the more clearly we realize the oneness of the spirit that dwells within.

Some people think that only they live truly, that they are everything, and that others are as nothing. These people have a narrow life and a grievous death, for when dying they feel that everything they are is dying. On the other hand, reasonable and good people realize that the life of others is as important as their own: they do not live in their "I" alone but in others. It is easy for these people to die, for they sense that their life in others remains. All works of love demonstrate to us that our true self is not only within our own personality, but also in all things living. If you live for yourself alone, you will think you are among enemies, you will feel that the happiness of others obstructs your own happiness. If you live for others you feel you are among friends, and the happiness of everybody else will be your own happiness. One who benefits another knows no separation from this other being, for the same being by which one lives is in all other beings, only in another form. Through love we can become one with other creatures and share their lives. If you live the life of the spirit, all disunion or conflict among people causes you spiritual suffering. In ceasing to respect other people, no matter how evil, unjust, stupid, or disagreeable they may be, you break connection not only with them, but also with the entire spiritual world. In order to live in peace with all, think of the common bond uniting you, and not of that which separates you from them.

4. Effects of realizing the oneness of the spirit in all human beings.

The same spirit exists in the souls of all humans as in our own. To the extent that we realize the oneness of the soul in all, new relations fostering peace, joy, and happiness are established among people. Love kindles love. God awakening within you awakes himself also in others. When meeting other people, no matter how disagreeable or repulsive they may seem to us, it is well to remember that through them we have the chance of communion with the spirit that lives in them, in ourselves, and the whole world; therefore we must not feel burdened by this interaction, but be grateful for it as a blessing. Quarreling with even one other person means cutting ourselves off from all of humankind. Not acknowledging that the same spirit dwells in all accounts for hatred, for the striking differences in personal wealth and resources, and for all human suffering.

CHAPTER FOUR

God

Where love is, God is.
from "Where Love Is, God Is"

Besides all that is physical within us and in the entire universe, we know something that is spiritual (non-physical) which gives life to our body and is connected with it. This we call our soul or spirit. The same non-physical something which gives life to everything, we call God (or the Spirit, the Supreme Being, Allah, the Higher Power, the Universal Principle).

1. God is known to us from within.

When we reflect on it, we realize that each of us is but a part of what is, and we start thinking that we are separated from the physical world. Further thought reveals instead that we feel separated from that which has neither beginning nor end in time or space, that is, from the spiritual, from God—that something in us without which we would be nothing. We know God within ourselves or not at all. We know not even ourselves, if we do not know God who animates us. We should love God and foster his presence within ourselves. Love and the ability to reason are the characteristics of God which we recognize within ourselves. Other things often are crowding our awareness of God; if only we make more space for God, our awareness of him will increase. A person can only truly love that in which there is no evil, and God alone is free of all evil. We speak of God in many ways, but all feel and understand him and his commands in the same way. We cannot help having faith in God. While we may have different forms of faith in God or no faith at all, without this faith we cannot understand ourselves. Although not knowing what they lack, individuals who have lost God are aware of lacking something that is necessary for life.

2. A rational person is bound to acknowledge God.

God dwells both in the limitless universe and in the human soul. Those who do God's will recognize that he chose to dwell in us for our blessedness. When we contemplate the wonders of the universe and the wonders of our own soul, we are contemplating God. At all times all peoples have believed in an invisible power (God, Spirit) that sustains the world. The visible world is a shadow of this invisible and eternal power, which is characterized by love and reason. It is there for all people to see, both in the world around them and in their own souls. If they think about it, they cannot help acknowledging that which we call God.

3. The will of God.

A person is to God as an infant is to its mother: the infant knows its mother as caregiver and sustainer, and loves her for it. So it is with us and God. The more we fulfill the will of God the better we know him. But we can never fully know God. The more we know God and the more we do his will, the better we will love others. I am God's instrument, his tool to use for a purpose, a purpose that is good and rational, but incomprehensible to me. I must serve God by silently doing his will.

4. God cannot be known by reason.

It is impossible to know God as he really is, and it is impossible to know him or to prove or disprove his existence by reason, but it is possible to feel God's presence within us. Strive to do God's will and to feel his presence within you more and more vividly. We cannot help but sense that there is a meaning and purpose in life. Every attempt of my imagination to comprehend God only puts me further away from him. Even the pronoun "he" somehow belittles or limits him. God cannot be expressed in words.

5. Disbelief in God.

Those who say there is no God are wrong. But they will always find ways to refute him if in their hearts they do not want to believe in him. For those who live wickedly, there is no God. God is God only to those who seek him. Those of a humble heart, whether they are clever or ignorant, and those who are truly wise may know God; proud people may not. If you seek God you will find him. Doubts do not mean that there is no God, only that something was wrong with your previous ideas about him. God's existence cannot and does not need to be proven. God simply is. Only the very pitiable and the very depraved deny him.

6. Loving God.

Only by loving God can a person love all equally. Many people do not understand what it means to love their neighbor, who may not be someone agreeable or useful to them. We should love all people equally, even those who may be most disagreeable and hostile. Loving one's neighbor is impossible without loving God, who is the same in all humans.

CHAPTER FIVE

Love

Love is life.
All, everything that I understand,
I understand only because I love.
from *War and Peace*

He now felt something
he had never before experienced—
the certainty that love is invincible.
from *Resurrection*

. . . mutual love is the fundamental law of human life.
from *Resurrection*

Human souls, separated bodily from one another and from God, strive to unite with that from which they are separated. The soul unites with God through a constantly growing consciousness of God within and with souls of others through showing love to them.

1. Love unites humans with God and with fellow creatures.

Jesus said we should love God with all our heart, soul, and mind, and our neighbor as ourselves. Only perfection can be loved fully. If we try to love that which is imperfect, sooner or later we will see our error and the love will cease. But the love of God, which is the love of perfection, cannot cease. We can unite only in God; therefore all must move in the direction of God. To love everyone seems difficult, but at first all things seem difficult until you learn how to do them. We can and must learn how to love all people. Do not ask God to unite you. He has made you one already by placing his one and the same spirit in you all. Only cast off the things which divide you, and you will be one.

Do not fear God; for he is love. You cannot love what you fear. Be conscious of him within you, and you will fear nothing in the world. From love nothing can come but good. Desire nothing but to love God. To be like God, you must fear nothing and desire nothing for self; to achieve this aim, practice only love. Love God and you will find what you seek.

2. Just as the human body craves food and suffers when deprived of it, so the human soul craves love and suffers when deprived of it.

All souls are drawn to God and to one another. So that we might live all as one, God revealed to us what we need by entering our souls and manifesting himself as love. The troubles of humanity come from our living our lives apart from one another, because we have no faith in that voice of love that dwells within us and draws us together. As long as we live the life of the body, we feel separated from others; it cannot be otherwise. But as soon as we start to live the life of the spirit, we don't want to be separated from others; we will strive to become one with them. And it is love alone that makes people one. The more we unite, the better we will live. The more I love others, the less I feel separated from them. Be one with people in things on which you agree; do not demand agreement in things on which you disagree. Love your enemies and you will have none.

3. Love is only genuine when it embraces all.

God wanted us to be happy; therefore he instilled in us a longing for happiness. He wanted us all to be happy together, not as individuals. We have all been born alike; we all seek our own good. We all understand it is better to help each other than to harm each other. The same love for each other has been implanted in our hearts. Hence we will be happy only when we all love one another. We are like stones joined in an arch, and are bound to collapse unless we support one another. The greatest good is to be in love and harmony with all people. If we only worked as hard to learn to love as we do to learn various crafts and sciences, we would soon train ourselves to love everyone, both those who attract us and those who repulse us. In genuine love we love not for our own benefit but for the benefit of others. On meeting a person, do not consider that person's usefulness to you, but yours to that person. We must respect everyone no matter how miserable, ridiculous, or repulsive that person may be, for the same spirit dwells in everyone.

Be good to all people as they are, not requiring them to change themselves (which they cannot do), nor requiring them to stop being themselves. Love is genuine only when it embraces all. A disagreement with another person is painful, but hatred is still more painful; because we are in discord with that which is one in all, we are in discord with ourselves. If we separate ourselves from others we will be weary, lonely, and despondent. Endeavor to love those whom you once did not love, whom you have condemned, or who may have done you an injury. If you succeed in doing so you will learn a new joy. The light of love will shine in your heart once it is rid of hatred.

4. Only the soul may be truly loved.

Loving only the body brings suffering. Instead we should love only the soul, which is the same in all people, and therefore we should love others. All people live by the same spirit. All are one and the same, but we are separated in this life by our bodies. If we realize that we all live by the same spirit, we must all unite in love. Do those things that unite people and avoid doing those things that separate them. The meaning of life is to make the soul more and more independent of the body and to bring it into union with the souls of others, and with the principle of all—God.

5. Love is a natural characteristic of humankind.

It is the law of our nature to love. Our most precious gift is our capacity to love. Helen Keller, who was deaf, dumb, and blind, was taught to read and write by the sense of touch; when her teacher tried to explain to her the meaning of love, the girl answered: "Yes, I understand, it is that which people feel one toward another." All faiths—Hindu, Jewish, Buddhist, Chinese, Christian, Muslim, and others—teach that the most necessary thing in the world is to learn to love. Five centuries before Jesus, the Chinese sage Mi-Ti taught that humanity should respect love alone, not power, wealth, or courage. A time must come when humanity will cease to fight, and when people will love one another. Let us therefore do all within our power to hasten the coming of this time.

6. Love alone brings true blessing.

If we seek what is good, we will receive it only if we seek
what is good for all, and love alone can give this. Let us not
love in word, but in deed and truth. If we look within
ourselves, we discover the spirit of God. If we recognize this
spirit within us, we shall love others, and if we love others
we shall receive all that our heart desires: we shall be happy.
Material blessings and pleasures of all kinds are obtained
only at the cost of robbing others. Spiritual benefits and the
blessing of love are obtained by increasing the happiness of
others. Modern technology may be useful for bringing people together, thus hastening the Kingdom of God; without
love, however, machines do not unite but divide people
further apart.

If we stopped in order to look within ourselves, we should
discover the spirit of God and the principle of true happiness: our love for one another. Krishna said, "Do not look
upon the world and the deeds of men, but gaze into your
own soul and you will find therein that blessing which you
seek where it is not. You will find love. Having found love,
you will see that this blessing is so great that, possessing it,
you will not crave anything else."

Love all those with whom you come in contact, and be
content, come what may, and you will have nothing to fear
or desire. Some say "What is the sense of doing good to
others if they repay evil for good?" If you love those to
whom you do good, you have already received your reward
in your love for them, and you will receive a still greater
reward if you bear in love that evil which they repay you. If
a good deed is performed with some end in view, it is no
longer a good deed. True love is love without knowing why
or for what purpose. Hate even just one person, and all the
joys of love will leave your soul. If you love others, you have

received from God life's supreme blessing—love. The time will come that Jesus spoke of, a time when we will no longer be proud of gaining by force power over others and the fruits of their labors, and when we will rejoice not in arousing fear and envy, but will be proud of loving all people. Then we will cherish that feeling of love which makes us overlook injuries inflicted upon us by others. Love gives, but seeks nothing in return.

CHAPTER SIX

Faults, Temptations, Superstitions

*I sit on a man's back, choking him
and making him carry me, and yet
assure myself and others that I am very sorry for him
and wish to ease his lot by all possible means
—except by getting off his back.*
from *What Then Must We Do?*

Human life would be an unceasing source of blessings if superstitions, temptations, and faults (sins) did not deprive people of the capacity of enjoying these blessings. Faults consist in indulging bodily passions. Temptations are incorrect ideas of our relation to the world. Superstitions are false beliefs accepted as part of religion.

1. True life is not in the body , but in the spirit.

A fault is failing to guide the body in the right direction (just as one guides the plow in the right furrow); the body slips, missing doing what it ought. The person who has corrupted his soul through a life of indulging the body loses the capacity to seek happiness in love. Improve your soul, free yourself from faults, temptations, and superstitions. There are two conflicting voices within everyone. One says, "Eat of it yourself," and the other, "give him to eat who asks;" one says, "avenge," the other, "forgive;" one says, "believe what is told you," the other, "think for yourself." Happy is the person who has trained to hear the voice of the spirit and not the voice of the body. Humans may waste their energy overeating, or overindulging in sex, or seeking power or fame, whereas we need only one thing—to cultivate our spirit. You cannot at the same time pay heed to your spirit and to worldly benefits; if you would save your soul, give up worldly benefits. In order to attain greater freedom, people build themselves a prison out of their faults, temptations, and superstitions, and confine themselves therein of their own free will. Instead, the purpose of life is to bring our souls to full growth, and to establish the spiritual kingdom on earth. We can do both by releasing within ourselves that light of the spirit which was put into our souls.

2. What are faults?

The Buddhists count the following as faults or sins: murder, theft, adultery, drunkenness, and lying. Humans are not punished *for* their faults, but by the faults themselves, for each new fault removes a person further away from love and true happiness. The entire life of a human consists in ridding oneself of faults; therefore, only in this freedom from faults is the true blessedness of life.

3. Temptations and superstitions.

Faults hinder the manifestation of love within us. Thus a
human need do just one thing to fulfill the will of God: rid
oneself of faults. Reason separates humans and animals, but
there are those who use reason to find excuses for the evil
deeds that bring them pleasure. This is what leads humans
into the temptations and superstitions from which the world
suffers. Do not think you are without faults, nor that you are
born and will die in faults, and hence need not labor within
yourself. Both delusions are equally harmful. A person's self
has two parts: the body and the soul. Although some grow
into the habit of serving their bodies against the wishes of
their souls, the latter will always conquer. Faults are at first a
stranger in your soul, then a guest, and when faults become
your habit, they are your master.

Young people begin life on unfamiliar paths, and on each
side they find byways that seem more pleasant to follow.
Soon, however, they find that they have lost their way and
stray further to their ruin. There are two ways to go when
one is guilty of a fault: one is to acknowledge the fault and
try not to repeat it; the other is to mistrust conscience and to
inquire what people think of such a fault, and, if they do not
condemn it, to continue with the fault, without realizing the
evil of it. The recognition of truth is not in itself sufficient
to turn people from evil and to draw them toward good.
People will understand truth when they are brought to the
ultimate degree of delusion and the suffering that results
from it.

A well-dressed person avoids mud, but once that person's
clothes are soiled fewer precautions are taken. Eventually,
after the clothes are badly soiled, a person will walk boldly
through the mud, accumulating more with each step. This is
what happens with a person gradually becoming soiled by

faults. Do not follow this example. Were you guilty of a fault? Be sorry, and avoid faults all the more. Faults are of the body; temptations come from thoughts of people; and superstitions from the distrust of one's reason.

4. The main task of our life is ridding ourselves of faults, temptations, and superstitions.

It is possible for people to live together only because they know their weaknesses and struggle against faults, temptations, and superstitions. A human's life consists in being more and more free from faults. Work toward such freedom in your life, and you will be happy. Nothing can free one from faults. One can only realize one's fault and strive not to repeat it. If you refuse to fight faults, you shirk the principal task of life. A person's soul is filled with love, but that love will not show itself if faults are also present. Deliver your soul from what chokes it, and you will love everybody, even those you have hated. Humans are conscious at the same time of the animal and of God within, and therefore cannot be without fault. Neither children nor saints are free from fault: a child may have fewer faults than others, as may a saint, but each has faults nevertheless, for there is no life without faults. To combat faults, stop doing the things to which you are accustomed. This will show whether you are master of your body or whether it is master of you.

5. The significance of faults, temptations, and superstitions for the manifestation of spiritual life.

Struggling with and overcoming faults, temptations and superstitions gives meaning and joy to life. But for faults, humanity would not know the joy of righteousness. If we had no soul, we would not know the faults of the body. And without these faults, we would not know that we had a soul.

We make use of the experience of those who came before us in distinguishing good from evil, and in following the path of struggle against evil. We move boldly down this path, a path ever obstructed by faults, temptations, and superstitions that whisper to us that there is no need to seek anything, and that we should live just as we happen to live. Faults, temptations, and superstitions are the soil that covers the seeds of love so that these seeds may spring into life.

FAULTS

CHAPTER SEVEN

Overindulgence

---

*He had formed luxurious habits which he could not
easily give up . . . He looked at the luxurious fittings
of his studio with a heavy heart . . .
[His house was decorated] with all the expensive
luxury that indicates the possession of much idle
money [money acquired without labor] . . .*

from *Resurrection*

The only true happiness is in love. But we lose this
happiness when, instead of developing the love within
us, we develop and indulge the appetites of our bodies.

1. All that is superfluous is harmful to the body and to the soul.

To use one's reason to invent pleasures for the body is wrong. If you want to live a life of peace and freedom, learn not to crave that which you can do without. All that the body needs is easily obtained. Only the unnecessary things are difficult to get. The more you accustom yourself to luxury, the more you become a slave, because the more things you require, the more you lose your freedom. Perfect freedom is needing nothing at all, and next to it is needing very little. Indulging the body too much is a sure way to weaken it. A happy life is not achieved by humoring the body to excess; gluttony, intoxication, overdressing, and undue use of adornments do not lead to happiness; reducing one's needs does.

2. The whims of the body cannot be fully satisfied.

Little is needed to sustain the body's basic needs, while the whims of the body have no end. It is relatively easy to provide basic food and clothing, but no power can obtain all the things that a person may crave. Humoring the flesh and giving it more things than it needs is a grievous error, because a life of luxury lessens rather than increases enjoyment from food, recreation, sleep, home, and clothes. In addition, many luxuries can only be obtained by directly or indirectly making others do for us what we can do ourselves.

3. The fault or error of gluttony.

If we ate only when hungry, and then only simple, clean, wholesome food, we would know no illness and could resist passions more easily. Food which a person requires to be healthy and able to work is simple to prepare, inexpensive, and found everywhere (bread, fruits, roots, water). Delicacies such as ice cream or pastries are not only more difficult to prepare but also are directly harmful to the body. Eat to live, do not live to eat. Overeating decreases physical energy.

4. The fault of eating meat for food.

Since ancient Greece, philosophers (such as Pythagoras) taught people that they can fully satisfy themselves by eating grains, herbs, fruits and vegetables, and abstaining from the practice of capturing, butchering, and eating living creatures. The people did not listen to the philosophers, but now more people are giving up the overindulgence of eating meat. "Thou shalt not kill" does not apply only to killing human beings, but also to killing any living creature. The happiness which we receive from feelings of compassion and mercy toward animals will make up for the pleasure lost through not hunting or not eating meat.

5. Drugging oneself with wine, tobacco, opium, etc.

To live right, we need, above all, to exercise our reason. Therefore, dulling our reason by drugging ourselves with such drugs as tobacco, wine, whisky, and opium is wrong. By smoking, drinking alcohol, and partaking of other drugs, humans extinguish the only light that they have—their reason. Overeating leads to laziness, using intoxicating drinks leads to sexual unrestraint. Wine, opium, and tobacco, which are unnecessary for our life, drug or stupefy us into forgetting that we lack the things we would like to have. Drinking or smoking has never inspired anyone to good deeds such as work, meditating on an issue, looking after a sick person, or praying; using drugs (including alcohol) dulls the senses and thus often leads to all sorts of crimes.

6. Overindulging the body is injurious to the soul.

Pampering the body with too many unnecessary things deprives others of necessities. Luxurious dwellings, apparel, and food waste the resources that would meet the needs of many. Accustoming ourselves to luxuries forces us to labor more to satisfy our cravings for such luxuries. Some of this extra labor is forced, often through craftiness, onto the shoulders of others. Muhammad, the founder of Islam, pointed out that excess of food and drink destroys a person's heart. The New Testament saying, "Where your treasure is, there will your heart be also," points out that if we view our bodies as our treasure, we will do all we can to provide them with dainty food, pleasant accommodation, fine apparel, and amusements. The more strength we use to serve the body, the less we have for our spiritual life.

7. He alone is free who is master of the desires of his body.

Some think happiness is found in fancy food, rich apparel, and luxuries of all sorts. But Socrates said that to desire nothing is the greatest happiness, and we must train ourselves to want little in order to approach that highest degree of happiness. The less we indulge the body in matters of food, clothing, housing, and amusement, the more free our lives will be. No one has ever regretted choosing to live simply. It is better to be poor than rich, because the rich are more bound up in faults than the poor. The rich who train their children in the ways of gluttony, luxury, and inactivity or apathy corrupt them and store up great suffering for them.

Only the body can suffer; the spirit knows no suffering. If you would not suffer, live more for the spirit and less for the body. One is free only through mastering the desires of the body.

CHAPTER EIGHT

Sexual Unrestraint

. . . marriage without love is not marriage;
love alone sanctifies marriage;
real marriage is only such as is sanctified by love.
from *The Kreutzer Sonata*

In all people, men and women alike, dwells the Spirit of God. Every woman in relation to a man should be first of all a sister, and every man to a woman, a brother. We should first see in someone a fellow human being also endowed with a spark of the same Spirit, rather than a sexual partner.

1. The need to strive after sexual restraint.

According to St. Paul, those who are not married are able to care for matters that belong to God and how to please him; but those who are married care for the things of the world and how husband and wife may please each other. Although few people may practice complete restraint, anyone can strive to practice relative restraint. Pointing to perfection as a goal toward which we must strive does not mean that we shall reach it. It is not given to us to attain perfection, but to strive after it. Besides, sexual restraint is a useful way to help curb the unavoidable population explosion.

2. The fault of uncontrolled sexual craving.

People use the same word, "love," when referring to spiritual love (the love of God and fellow humans) as they do when referring to sexual love. This is a mistake. There is a great difference between the two. The law of God is to love God and your neighbor—that is, everyone—without distinction. In sexual love, a man loves an individual woman above all others, and a woman, an individual man; this is a relationship with a more limited focus.

Besides, we should be cautious of unrestrained sexual activity, as it often keeps people from fulfilling their mission as beings endowed with a spirit within.

3. Misery caused by lack of sexual restraint.

A moth rushes to the flame because it does not realize it will burn its wings; a fish swallows the worm on the hook because it does not know that the hook means ruin for it. But we humans know that lustful passions (unrestrained sexual involvements) will surely entrap us, and still we yield to them. Just as fireflies over a swamp lead people astray into the mire, and are lost to view themselves, even so the delights of uncontrolled sexual infatuation or gratification deceive us. People go astray, their lives are ruined, and when they come to their senses and look around, that which has ruined their lives is often but a puff of smoke where there was fire.

4. Criminal attitude of our governments toward sexual unrestraint.

The situation of women who earn a living from indiscriminate sex is condoned and regulated by certain governments. Sex without marriage has led to the formation of a group of women (prostitutes) whose bodies and souls are ruined for the gratification of men.

5. Fighting the fault of extreme sexual craving and unrestraint.

As an animal, the human being has to fight with other creatures and multiply to increase the species. But as a creature endowed with love and reason, a human being must not fight with other creatures, and must love them all equally. We must not multiply in order to increase our species, but practice restraint. Every man should treat every woman as his sister, and every woman should treat every man as her brother. When a man and a woman get married, they must still practice a certain amount of sexual restraint, viewing each other as spiritual partners. The principal weapon in combating sexual unrestraint is our realization of our spirituality. We must only remember what we are in order to see sexual unrestraint for what it is. Struggling with sexual unrestraint is the most difficult of all combats. All passions are born of thought and then are sustained by it, but no passion is sustained and nourished so much as sexual unrestraint. Do not dwell on sexual cravings, but repel them.

6. Marriage.

In order to attain a goal, one must aim beyond it. To help both marriage partners to remain faithful to each other, it is necessary for both to have an ideal of relative restraint. Many think that in married life it is permissible to engage in unrestrained sex, but the opposite is true: with marriage comes the need to strive even harder to practice restraint. Current thinking is that all human beings, male and female, must marry without fail; on the contrary, every human being must endeavor to practice restraint as much as possible so as to give oneself fully to the service of God. If marriage is looked upon as releasing us from the necessity of striving after restraint or chastity, then marriage, instead of curtailing lust, encourages it. Unfortunately this is the attitude toward marriage of the majority of people. As a matter of fact, to bind your life with that of another in a sexual relationship should be based on an earnest mutual commitment and is a matter of great import.

7. Children are the price we pay for sex.

The purpose of marriage is to have children. People who marry for this reason feel that by having children, they have transferred some of their obligations onto their children. There is a consciousness that lends a spiritual significance both to married life and the bringing up of children—the consciousness that if I have fallen short in yielding myself entirely to the service of God, I can do everything in my power to enable my children to do what I failed to do. Children are like an outpouring of innocence and freshness which both ensures the well-being of the species, and helps render human nature less corrupt and depraved. Through childhood we have a glimpse of paradise here on earth.

The significance of bearing children is lost for people who

engage in unbridled sexual activity and view love merely as a means of physical gratification. For such people, instead of being the purpose and the justification of marital relations, children become a hindrance to an agreeable continuance of pleasures, and therefore both in and out of marriage the use of contraceptives has grown.

Male and female animals have intercourse only when young can result, but humans do so for pleasure without thinking whether it will lead to the birth of children or not. As things stand, pleasure needs to be accompanied by responsibility for the birth and growth of our children. Therefore, it is our business to fulfill all the obligations which the presence of children imposes upon us.

CHAPTER NINE

Freeloading

. . . those who devise and prepare
for the plunders and murders [perpetrated by
the military] and who compel the working people
to carry them out, are but an insignificant minority,
who live in luxury and idleness
upon the labor of the workers.
from "Carthage is to be Destroyed"

It is unjust to receive from people more than the labor which you give them. But since you cannot tell whether you give more than you receive, and since at any moment you may lose your ability to give, work for others as much as you can while you have the strength, and take from them as little labor as possible. Unjustly availing ourselves of the labors of others is freeloading.

1. Availing oneself of the labors of others, without personally laboring, is a grievous fault.

To waste, spoil, or destroy any product of human labor is to waste labor and sometimes human life. Christian morality instructs us to consider ourselves as brothers and sisters and therefore to first: cease inducing others to labor for us; and second: reduce to a minimum our use of the labor and products of others. We should not let another do for us what we can do for ourselves. It is beneficial for a rich person to live as a laborer even for a short time in order to realize the wrongfulness of the life of the rich, for living in luxury prevents the rich from loving others. This is so because the things which the rich use were made by the economically weaker individuals whom they compel to render them service. Such service is rendered unwillingly, through sheer necessity, and frequently with much resentment. Loving others means first getting off their backs and ceasing to oppress them.

People usually think that cooking, sewing, and looking after children is a woman's job, and men feel embarrassed doing it. On the contrary, it is shameful for a man to be engaged in trifles or to be idle while his pregnant wife, tired and often weak, is over-exerting herself cooking, doing laundry, and tending the children. We should support ourselves with our own labor. Even a monk engaged in spiritual tasks should support himself by his own labor rather than count on others to support him.

2. It is not a hardship, but a joy, to obey the command to labor.

Labor is the unquestionable law of the life of the body; love is the law of the life of the spirit. Without a sound body, one that can and does labor, there can be no sound spirit. It is not a hardship, but a joy, to obey the command to labor: "In the sweat of thy brow shalt thou earn thy daily bread." Rather than this command being truth because it is in the Bible, it is in the Bible because it is a universal law of life. Idleness (or breaking that law of the life of the body) makes people dissatisfied and cross. The soul cannot live the highest life of the spirit when the body is idle. Eating the bread earned by another's labor deprives one of the joy of labor. If we release ourselves from the law of labor, we destroy ourselves through the weakening and decaying of our bodies; if we release ourselves from that law by compelling others to labor for us, we damage our own souls. Do not let your labor seem burdensome, seek no praise for it. Labor, if performed for others with love, benefits the soul. The rich have more things and less joy from such things; the poor have fewer things, but more joy.

3. The best toil is tilling the soil.

Manual labor and, particularly, tilling the soil is good not only for the body, but also for the soul. Those who do not labor with their hands cannot have a sound idea of things. Such people are forever thinking, speaking, listening, or reading. Their minds have no rest, are excited, and easily wander. Agricultural labor, on the other hand, is useful because it is restful and enables us to realize simply, clearly, and reasonably our place in life. Peasants are not educated enough to reason incorrectly.

4. What is known as division of labor is merely an excuse for idleness.

Success in production has been attributed to the division of labor when in fact it is human beings, rather than labor, who have become divided. There are those who in their quest to be free have become slaves to this system; these people act like machines, not understanding the true meaning of freedom. They labor and do not enjoy their work, and see wealth as the only source of pleasure. They resent those who have wealth and did not work for it. There are three ways to obtain riches: by labor, begging, or theft. Those who do not labor are therefore beggars or thieves. There are three types of thieves: those who don't care and will remain thieves, those who do care but feel they have no choice, and those who care and also try to reform.

5. The activities of those who do not obey the law of labor are always futile and fruitless.

All humans have a duty and obligation to use their hands and feet to do work in order not to perish from hunger and cold. This work should not be to excess, should not drain them of their strength or ruin their bodies; rather it should be a pleasure, good for the soul. The amusements and activities of idlers not only ruin their souls but also interfere with and burden those who labor. People who do not labor have much more time to seek pleasure, and do so because they feel the emptiness of their life but do not realize the emptiness of the momentary whims that attract their fancy.

6. The harm of idleness.

One must not be ashamed of any labor but of idleness instead. Respect people for the work they do, not for their position or wealth. Those who do not labor must either crawl before others or use force upon them. The poor envy the rich and the rich envy the poor. The former because their basic needs are not met and the latter because the moment individuals have others do their work they enter upon a life of idleness where doubts, melancholy, sorrows, lack of compassion, and despair await them. The poor are better off, for frequently they are not to blame for their poverty, but the rich always have themselves to blame for their wealth and idleness.

CHAPTER TEN

Greed

[After Pahom's death] his servant dug a grave
long enough for Pahom to lie in.
Six feet from his head to his heels
was all he needed.

from "How Much Land Does a Man Need?"

The fault of greed (covetousness) is in securing many things or money of which others are in need, and in hoarding these in order to use at will the labor of others.

1. The fault of wealth.

Wealth promotes greed, whereas a modest life promotes giving and sharing. In addition, the presence of wealth necessitates the presence of poverty—the suffering and labor of the poor—to provide the rich with excessive luxury. The poor are most easily exploited. In the kingdom of truth, which Jesus preached, there are neither rich nor poor. Honest people are not usually rich. Rich people are not usually honest. Wealth is a great fault before God, poverty is a great fault before people.

2. Owning land is a crime.

Every person has the right to utilize the land for making a living; to deny anyone that right is absurd because no one can own the land or sell it. Land is the property of all generations and of all those who labor upon it.

3. Harmful effects of wealth.

Poverty and need give people firmness and strength, whereas wealth leads to laziness, madness, and dull wit. The rich may never live in peace because they are constantly worried that their wealth may disappear, and because their duties and obligations increase with wealth. Also, they feel they may only associate with those who are richer, or as rich as they, lest they be forced to confront their faults and feel shame. The life of the rich, freed from the obligation to labor, cannot but be crazy. If people only knew how much good they lose while seeking wealth, they would seek to be rid of it. Wealth does not bring us happiness, but it spoils our lives and the lives of others.

4. We should not envy wealth, but be ashamed of it.

Rich people are not to be honored or envied, but to be avoided and pitied. The rich need not boast of wealth, but ought to feel ashamed of it. The envy of the poor for riches is as bad as the self-contentment of the rich. The rich must realize their own fault before they criticize the poor for their envy, and the poor must realize the fault of their envy and jealousy before they criticize the rich.

5. Excuses for wealth.

If one is receiving an income without laboring for it, someone is laboring without getting paid for it. Only those convinced that they are better than others can calmly enjoy riches while surrounded by those living in poverty. People are tempted to view that which they enjoy as good; they close their eyes to the evil involved. To a true Christian, wealth is an evil and a shame. To say "rich Christian" is like saying "warm ice." The science of political economy (as practiced in capitalistic societies) was invented to soothe and calm troubled minds and consciences, so that rich people could enjoy their wealth without feeling guilty about robbing from the poor.

6. For our own good, we should pay heed not to the increase of our possessions, but to the increase of love within us.

Those living a life of love can neither try to increase their wealth nor keep it. Material treasures are perishable, but spiritual treasures last forever. Happiness depends on the spirit within us and not on our material wealth. Material wealth hinders the progress of the spirit.

7. Combating the fault of greed.

The only joy that may be obtained from riches is the joy of giving them away. Love must accompany such deeds. To escape poverty, one must merely diminish one's wishes. The worst thief is not one who takes what he needs, but one who hoards what he does not need—things unnecessary to self but useful to others. One may either work for the earthly life or for God, but not for both.

CHAPTER ELEVEN

Anger

The first law [Gospel According to Matthew,
Chapter 5] *is that man should not kill,
and should not even be angry with his brother; and
should not consider anyone "worthless" . . .*

from *Resurrection*

The worst of all faults are those which separate us from others—envy, fear, condemnation, enmity, anger—in general ill-will toward others. These faults hinder love from uniting the human spirit with God and others.

1. What is the fault of ill will?

If you feel gloomy or irritable, you know that something is wrong; you either love that which you ought not to love or do not love that which you ought to love. The faults of overeating, idleness, and sexual unrestraint are evil, but also lead to another, worse fault—ill will, or an unloving attitude toward others. Dreadful are the feelings of people who hate one another, more dreadful than even robberies and murders, and so is the hatred felt by people, that causes them to rob and kill.

2. The senselessness of anger.

Ill will comes from folly: I am angry because people have done what they need to do and not what I want them to do. Is this not foolishness? People who are spiritually blind imagine that whatever happens to them is done against them with evil intent, so they are angry with others, failing to realize that their woes are not due to other people, but due to their blindness. The higher a person's self opinion, the more that person is annoyed with others. The more humble a person is, the more kindly and less prone to anger. If you can forgive and learn to love someone who has injured you, you are doing the highest thing that a person can aspire to. You may be unable to refrain from anger when offended or insulted; but you can always refrain from showing in word and deed what is in your heart. Spite always comes from powerlessness. If a person scolds or insults you, do not be upset, do not respond in kind, do not do as that person does.

3. Anger against our brothers and sisters is unreasonable because the same Spirit dwells in all.

When you criticize someone, remember that the spirit of God dwells within that person. If I realize that only that is evil to me which I commit myself, no evil person can harm me or compel me to do evil. And if I remember that every person is my neighbor, and that God dwells within all of us, then I cannot be angry with anyone, for we have all been created for one another. How then can I turn away from my neighbor, if contrary to his true nature, he commits evil against me? If you lived the life of the Spirit, no one could harm you, because the Spirit cannot be harmed or made angry, and it is within you. To live in harmony with people, remember when you meet someone that the Spirit which dwells within both of you only requires that you accept each other. Remember this when a feeling of unkindness rises within you, and you will immediately be delivered from this feeling. If you despise a person, you fail to value the good that is in that person. If you honor another beyond measure, you require too much. Esteem a person as someone in whom dwells the Spirit.

4. The less we think of ourselves, the kinder we are.

The better we are, the more gentle and kind we are toward all people. This is because good people remember that they also have been guilty of faults, and if they should be angry with others for being bad, they must be first angry with themselves. A thief or a mean person is someone gone astray, who is deprived of the greatest blessing, which is the knowledge of how to live in accord with reason and one's conscience. Such people should be pitied, not treated with anger. You might say that such people ought to be punished, but if our eyes are diseased and our sight is lost, you will not say that we must be punished for it. Pity such unfortunates and see that their errors do not arouse your anger.

If you say that evil people are all around you, it is a sure sign that you are very bad yourself. The wiser and more kindly we are, the more good we will see in others, and the more foolish and unkind we are, the more defects we will see in others. It is true that it is difficult to be kind to wicked people and liars, but these are just the people with whom we should be very kind, both for their sake and for our own. It is well to pity the poor and help them; it is still better not to judge the depraved, but to pity them also. The poor are suffering in their bodies, but the deceivers, drunkards, thieves, and murderers are suffering in that which is their most precious possession—their spirits. It is only by reason that we may convince a person of an error. As soon as we understand why someone does something we had considered evil, we will be unable to be angry, just as one cannot be angry with a stone for falling to the ground instead of upwards.

5. Love is necessary in our relationships with other people.

Do not associate with people if you feel no love towards them. People cannot be handled without love, any more than bees can without caution. If you treat people without love you will harm both them and yourself. If others offend us, that is their business, but our business is to do that which we consider good, to do unto others as we would have them do unto us. Do not be angry, or criticize others, but work to correct the evil that you see. This evil cannot be removed by your irritation, but only by the exercise of good will to all humans. You may judge another's actions, but love that person just the same.

It is also important to train yourself not to think evil of another, not to let ill will enter your thoughts. You might think that people's reason should help them to recognize their faults and to correct them. However, you also have the ability to reason to help you decide not to be angry with others because of their faults. Rather, awaken their conscience by rational and kind treatment, without anger, impatience, or haughtiness. There are those, however, who love to be angry. They are pleased with an opportunity to confuse and to insult anyone who deals with them. Remember that these are unfortunate people, strangers to the joy of a good disposition, and they should be pitied. May God guard you from pretending to love and to have compassion if you feel no love or compassion. This is worse than hatred.

6. Combating the fault of ill will.

If you know your weakness you will not be angry when others point it out. It may seem unkind of them, but they are helpful to you by doing this. There is only one way to keep from hating those who injure us; it is by doing good to them. Though you may be unable to change them, you can curb yourself. Muhammad taught that when you have an angry word on the tip of your tongue, you should not say it, but gulp it down. All people do what they think is best for them. If they are in error and do instead that which is worst for them, they should be pitied, but you should not be angry with them. Let us remember that we shall all return to the soil, and let us be meek and gentle.

7. Ill will harms most of all the person who harbors it.

No matter how much harm anger causes to others, it is most harmful to that person who harbors it. Anger is always more harmful than that which has provoked it. As opposed to injuring people for self-benefit, which is what a miser does, the angry person's behavior consists in injuring others without any benefit to self.

Do no harm even to enemies; herein is great virtue.

Poverty is no justification for evil, for evil leads only to greater poverty.

Let a person who would not live in grief and sorrow do no harm to others. You think that the object of your wrath is your enemy, yet your own wrath, which has entered your heart, is your principal enemy. Therefore make peace, and put out of your heart that painful feeling. A Hindu principle teaches that we should not quarrel, though we be offended and suffer; we should not give offence in word, deed, or thought for these rob us of our happiness. Earlier in my life I never permitted my anger to rise against those whom I considered to be above me. But the slightest act of a person whom I believed beneath me aroused my anger. Sometimes, even, the mere thought of a person's inferior position led me to insult that person. Thinking of self as being above others is one of the main causes of hostility among people.

TEMPTATIONS

CHAPTER TWELVE

Pride

---

*In order to obtain and hold power
a person must love it. Thus the effort to get it is
not likely to be coupled with goodness, but with the
opposite qualities of pride, craft and cruelty.*
from *The Kingdom of God Is Within You*

Freeing oneself from faults is at times difficult, mainly because faults find support in temptations. This is the case with pride, which is the temptation of thinking oneself superior to other people.

1. The senseless folly of pride.

Proud people think they are better and more important than other people. They are proud of things of which they should be ashamed: riches, glory, and honors. They are so busy teaching others that they have no time to think about themselves and their own faults. If you are stronger, wealthier, or more learned than others, strive to serve others from the over-abundance you have as compared with them. Proud people think that if they have what others lack, they need not share it with others, but only parade it before them. You are wrong to think you are superior to other people and can treat them differently from the way you would have them treat you. It is foolish for people to be proud of their bodies, but it is more foolish to be proud of their parents, ancestors, race, friends, or position in life. Much evil on earth is due to this foolish pride. It causes quarrels between individuals, families and nations. When two proud minds confront each other, they become angry because neither can be superior to the other.

We should not think of ourselves as wiser, nobler, or better than others because we cannot judge our own mind and virtue, and still less the true value of the minds and virtues of others. The more self-satisfied we are, the less reason there is to be satisfied.

2. National pride.

There are different types of pride: individual, family, group, and national. Pride is unrestrained self-love. To count oneself better than everyone else is wrong and foolish. To count one's family better than all others is worse, but to count one's nation better than all others is the greatest folly of all. Proud people do not consider this wrong, but think of it as a great virtue. We quarrel with others though we know it is wrong.

In order to deceive ourselves and drown the voice of our conscience (the small voice of the Spirit within us), we invent excuses for our hostility. One excuse is that we are better than others and they do not understand this. For this reason we have the right to be at odds with them. We use this excuse for ourselves, our families, our social class, and our nation. Nothing divides people so much as pride. Personal pride is harmful, but national pride is far more harmful. Millions upon millions of people died from it in the past and are still dying from it.

3. Human beings have no rational grounds for exalting themselves above others, as the same Spirit dwells in all people.

For those leading a spiritual life, no person is better than another, because the same soul dwells in all people. No individual should use any special titles when addressing another, such as "Sir," "Your Majesty," "Your Highness," etc. But the appropriate title for all is: "Brother" or "Sister." This title is good for the reason that it reminds us of the one Father in whom we are all brothers and sisters. Using that address reminds us that, because the same Spirit dwells in all people, it is wrong to think that there is even one person above us or one person beneath us. God is the only one who can judge us, because the valuable thing in humans is their spirit, and no one knows the value of the spirit but God.

4. Effects of the temptation of pride.

Pride defends not only itself but all the other faults. Pride monopolizes all our strength and shuts us off from the light of truth. The consciousness of faults is often more useful than good deeds, because the consciousness of faults makes one humble while a good deed frequently puffs up one's pride. In spite of all their merits and endeavors, proud people are not loved by others. There is no more repulsive characteristic than pride. The proud separate themselves from others and thus they are deprived of the greatest pleasure in life—a free and joyful association with all people.

5. Combating the temptation of pride.

The temptation of pride may be wiped out only by the recognition of the oneness of the Spirit that dwells in everyone. Having realized this, we can no longer count ourselves, or our family, or even our nation as better or higher than others. It is easy to live with others when you regard them neither as better and higher nor as worse and lower than yourself.

Proud people are like pedestrians walking on stilts instead of with their own feet. They are higher and the mud does not reach up to them and they take larger steps. But the trouble is that you cannot go very far on stilts and the chances are you will fall into the mud and people will laugh at you.

The main purpose of life is to improve your inner being, your self. But proud people consider themselves perfectly good. This is harmful for it hinders them from attending to that principal purpose of life, namely, making ourselves better.

CHAPTER THIRTEEN

Inequality

---

*. . . however gifted [you may be], however kind to
those around you, however circumstanced,
can you sit unmoved over your tea, your dinner,
your political, artistic, scientific, medical, or
educational affairs while you hear or see at your door
a hungry, cold, sick, suffering person? No.
Yet they are always there, if not at the door,
then ten yards or ten miles away.*
from "Industry and Idleness"

*. . . like those who are quite destitute of basic religious
feeling [which recognizes the equality and brotherhood
among all humans, he]
was fully convinced that the common people
were creatures entirely different from himself . . .*
from *Resurrection*

The spirit of God that dwells within us is the foundation
of our life. That spirit is one and the same in all people.
Therefore all are equal and cannot be separated into higher
or lower groups.

1. What the temptation of inequality is about.

In olden times it was believed that people were born of various races, and that some were meant to be masters and others to be slaves. People believed that this division was instituted by God. This was a crude and ruinous superstition. We need only to glance at the life of Christian nations to be amazed at the extent of inequality within them. Those professing the Christian faith, and particularly preaching equality, maintain an order of life which is striking in its cruel and obvious inequality. Some have fallen into the habit of dividing people in their mind into distinguished and obscure, noble and common, educated and uneducated, and they have grown so accustomed to this division that they really believe that some people are superior to others, that some people are to be more esteemed than others because they are classed by people in one group, while other people are classed in another group. Anyone treating groups of people differently cannot be truly religious. Many people today realize that inequality is a superstition, and in their hearts they condemn it. But those who profit from this inequality cannot make up their minds to give it up, while those who suffer from it do not know how to remove it.

2. The life of contemporary society is built on the inequality of people.

In their statements, educated and wealthy people often give the impression that they uphold equality for all and are indignant about oppression or lack of freedom of the working class. But the lives of these wealthy people are built on that oppression and lack of freedom, and they oppose any efforts of the working class to change these conditions. Those who inherit large fortunes or much land become so intoxicated with their luxury that they *cannot* put themselves in the place of a worker organizing a strike in their factories, or a poor peasant felling wood in their forests. If given a chance, such individuals without any hesitation will punish both the worker and the peasant.

3. Excuses for inequality.

Nothing leads to evil acts as much as people separating themselves into closed groups and cutting themselves off from others. Those who separate themselves from others and act superior to others bear some of the blame for inequality. But even more of the blame rests upon those who view themselves as inferior to the arrogant people who act superior. Christianity teaches that the same spirit dwells in all humans, which makes them brothers and sisters. Therefore the lives of all are equally sacred. Many people, however, believe that God divides humans into masters and slaves, believers and unbelievers, rich and poor. A choice was necessary between two things: either uproot one's entire way of life, or corrupt the teachings of Jesus. Most people have chosen the second course.

4. The superstition of patriotism.

It is foolish for people to think of themselves as better than others; it is still more foolish for a whole nation to consider itself better than other nations. Every person, before being a member of a particular nation, is a rational loving being, whose calling in this world is to love all people. Christians cannot help knowing that the distinction between their nation and others is an error, that their oneness with all the people in the world cannot be interrupted by frontier lines. They know that all people everywhere are brothers and sisters and are therefore equal. Regardless of class, faith, and nationality, a child meets another child with the same happy and friendly smile. But adults, who ought to know better than children, before meeting other people wonder to what class, faith, or nationality they belong, and adjust their attitude accordingly. No wonder Jesus said: "Be like little children."

5. All people are equal.

Equality is the recognition that all people in the world have the equal right to enjoy all the natural blessings of the world, an equal right to benefits of social life, and equal right to the respect of others. Laws which divide people into classes are a human invention which defeats the divine aim of the unity of all through the bonds of love.

At times we are dissatisfied with life because we do not see blessings where they are granted us. We are given the supreme joy of life—association with the people of the whole world—and we say: I want a peculiar blessing all to myself, to my family, to my nation. Everyone in this present age knows that all people have the same rights to the blessings of life, that no group of people is better or worse than another, and that all people are equal. Yet they live as though they do not know this.

6. Why are all people equal?

No matter who the people are, no matter what their fathers and grandfathers were, they are all alike as two drops of water because the spirit of God dwells in them. Only those who do not know that God dwells in them can count some people more important than others. To count all people equal to yourself does not mean that you are as strong, as skillful, as alert, as wise, as well educated, or as good as others; rather, it means that within you dwells the Spirit which also dwells in all other people.

7. The recognition of the equality of all people is feasible, and humanity gradually approaches this goal.

We cannot make a tall person equal to a short one, or a strong man equal to a weakling. Some people will always be stronger; some wiser than others. For this reason we need equal rights for all people. If, in addition to inequalities of mind and strength, there existed also inequalities of rights, the oppression of the weak by the strong would be even worse.

In your own life you can introduce equality among all people with whom you come in contact. Withhold undue respect from the so-called "great and mighty," and make it a point to show the same measure of respect to those considered unimportant and inferior.

8. They who live the life of the spirit count all people equal.

Jesus taught us what we have always known, that all people are equal because the same Spirit dwells within them. But since early times humankind has divided itself into classes. Although people know that they are equal, they live as though they did not know this, and assert inequality. Do not do this. Learn from children. The child treats the most important person in the land the same as an ordinary person. Do likewise. Meet all people with equal love and kindness. There can be no inequality in love. Love is only love when like the rays of the sun it falls equally upon all. When it falls upon some and excludes others, it is no longer love. It is difficult to love all people alike, but just because it is difficult should not stop us from striving after it. All that is good is difficult.

CHAPTER FOURTEEN

Force, or Violence

All violence consists in human beings,
by the threat of inflicting suffering or death,
coercing others to do what the coerced ones
do not wish to do.
from *The Law of Violence and the Law of Love*

One of the main causes of human misery is the wrong idea that some people may by force order or improve the lives of others.

1. The mistaken idea that some people may order the lives of others by force.

Improving yourself is a necessary and difficult task, requiring much moral effort, but the activity of those who think they can control the lives of others by force is futile, harmful, wicked, and vicious. People find it much easier to try to order the lives of others than their own, because if they fail, these others will suffer and not they themselves. Force brings no order into human life, but only disorder. When people say that all should live in peace, that no one should be injured, and yet they use force to compel others to live according to their will, it is as though they said, "Do as we say, but not as we do." Such people may be feared, but they cannot be trusted. Life cannot be improved by outside force, but only by our own effort. Some hold that using force is effective. But using force is responsible for terrible misery. Force, or violence, more than anything else, holds back the true progress of humankind toward perfection.

2. Conceptions of evil differ, and thus fighting evil with force or violence is not acceptable.

To fight one evil with another serves to increase, rather than to decrease, the amount of evil in the world. My use of force or violence to compel another person to do what I think is right legitimizes the use of force against me by a third person, even when our ideas of "right" differ. Jesus taught that since humans cannot establish beyond doubt what is evil, they must not use force to overcome that which they believe to be evil. By allowing the use of force to order the lives of others we condone such evils as torture, slavery, and war.

3. The ineffectiveness of force.

It is pointless to use force to stop people from doing evil

deeds, because they will not cease doing evil, but merely postpone such evil doing. Using force in this way merely instills in others resentment toward ourselves and toward what we believe is right. It is far better and more effective to persuade by word and reason. Using force or coercion usually results in failure. Even when force does prove successful, this is not evidence that this method is just. Submissiveness leads to dulling of the senses, and force leads to arrogance; but neither achieves true dignity.

4. Government is based on force.

Nothing is gained by the use of force to order lives, except making the human condition worse and spreading acceptance of the claim that good is achieved through force. The law of self-defence is indeed binding on animals, but we should choose to follow the law of human love—to return good for evil. Consider that in real life the causes of evil are usually the following:

a) the human error that an imaginary threat of attack is reason to commit real evil (the use of violence);

b) we are under the influence of the superstition about the lawfulness of using force.

Returning evil for evil is senseless and defeats its purpose.

5. Ruinous effects of the superstition of violence.

Jesus and other sages of the world have taught that rational human beings should repay evil with good. The evil of force used in so-called "self-defense" is worse than the evil defended against. Using force arouses resentment, and those who use it for self-defense not only fail as a rule to protect themselves, but even expose themselves to greater danger. Holding the view that some may by force order the lives of others, some people cease to distinguish good from evil, and are addicted to violence. That superstition about the use of force has led to the deterioration of Christianity. Violence is criminal, for it leads to murder. Nothing so delays the establishment of peace on earth as trying to bring it about by force, which is the opposite of peace.

6. Not using force to resist evil is the only way to replace the law of violence with the law of love.

Jesus taught us not to oppose force with force. But contrary to that teaching, the superstitious belief in forceful reorganization and control of life in society has taken root in our midst. Viewing the government as a reasonable and always legitimate source of power should be denounced as a superstition. For one thing, the laws of a human government vary from one country to another, from one generation to another. It is necessary not to obey the current government when its orders are opposed to divine law. But it is always right to obey divine law. Taking distance from our government may mean practicing some form of anarchy, not anarchy in the sense of the absence of institutions, but as the absence of those institutions through which constraint is used to make people submit.

Human life can change for the better only as a result of inner spiritual change, and never as the result of force used by some upon others. We have no right to try to order the lives of others. Only by striving after our own inner perfection can we influence the life of others. We have power only over ourselves. Humans are rational beings, and therefore can live by the guidance of reason and will eventually substitute free agreement for the use of force. Each act of force postpones this. Only by perfecting and improving our own selves can we improve the common life. The security and happiness of all is assured only by the morality of each of us. This morality is based on love which excludes force.

7. The corruption by many churches of Jesus' commandment regarding not using force to resist evil.

Force still reigns in society because the things preached in Jesus' name are not his teachings. People unwilling to change the familiar order of life simply distort or deny his commandment to return love for evil. Those calling themselves Christians wish to conceal from themselves and from others his teachings because the established order of life is profitable for them. They teach that his commandment of non-resistance to evil is non-binding, and yet this commandment is inseparably bound up with his entire teaching. For this reason alone the world continues to lead a pagan life. Even after accepting the principle that the meaning of life is found in love, some people still resist the message of love and nonviolence. The teaching of Jesus is that it is wrong to do evil to another person under any circumstances, whether as repayment for evil, for protection, or in order to save the life of another.

CHAPTER FIFTEEN

Punishment

He asked a very simple question:
"Why, and by what right, do some people lock up, torment,
exile, flog, and kill others, while they are themselves
just like those whom they torment, flog, and kill?"
from *Resurrection*

"Vengeance is mine; I will repay" (says the Lord).
from *The Bible*, quoted in *Anna Karenina*

The only means of salvation . . . is for us to acknowledge
ourselves to be guilty before God, and therefore
unable to punish or reform others . . .
from *Resurrection*

Unlike animals (who repay evil with evil), humans, being able to reason, cannot help seeing that evil increases evil, and they should therefore refrain from repaying evil with evil. But often the animal nature within us gains the upper hand over reason. We use reason (that should keep us from returning evil for evil) as an excuse to commit an evil which we call punishment.

Editor's Note: Here, after rejecting existing practices of punishment as meted out by government, Tolstoy does not discuss the necessity for society to confine serial killers, terrorists, and psychopaths in order to protect citizens from considerable harm. Tolstoy's disciple, Gandhi, explicitly acknowledged the need for society to protect its members from criminals. It seems that Tolstoy implicitly assumes there is such a need for non-punitive confinement.

1. Punishment never achieves its object.

It is untrue that punishment corrects people. Punishment (repaying evil with evil) is motivated by the desire to avenge oneself. Punishment is considered by some as being "instructive"—but it fails to teach, for teaching occurs only through kindness. Punishment only immerses us deeper in the animal nature. The reflex to snap back and return hurt for hurt is experienced by animals, and is also characteristic of the lowest stage of human development. These days, government leaders are practicing the same primitive behavior and taking on the responsibility to administer punishment. Humans, being endowed with reason, cannot help seeing that evil increases evil, and should therefore refrain from repaying evil with evil. The superstition that evil may be eliminated through punishment is harmful. For our stage of development, jail sentences are as cruel as punishment by whiplash a century ago. Besides, punishment is always cruel. Misguided people mistakenly projected on to God their own wish for vengeance (punishing certain people for their bad deeds). This is wrong—God is all love and is incapable of seeking vengeance.

Punishment is the most ignoble of all human actions. A science of punishment (criminal law) is fit only for the lowest stage of human development.

2. The superstitious belief in the reasonableness of punishment is reinforced by so-called criminal law.

The belief that punishment improves people is a superstition. Only a change in the inner, spiritual life of an individual can change him: the evil some inflict upon others does not improve anyone. Jesus said, "Let him who is without sin cast the first stone." No one has the right to condemn others. Though people find many reasons for imposing punishment, they always punish because they think it profitable for themselves. But the threat of penalty does not lessen evil; threats only increase the craving for evil. Institutional efforts to punish people for breaking criminal law hinder us from paying due attention to moral self-improvement (the only remedy to criminal behavior). I can only improve my own life, not that of others. The appearance of order exists in society not because there are penalties, but in spite of them. Punishment corrupts those who punish.

3. Retribution in personal relations.

Those who have committed evil are punished by the loss of peace within, and if they do not feel pangs of conscience, no imposed punishment will help. Punishment cannot destroy evil; only love frees one from evil. To punish is to abandon reason. We learn to return evil for evil from childhood. By instilling the idea that punishment may be just and beneficial, we do more harm than good to the child—who later punishes others. This process continues the idea that punishment is beneficial.

4. Retribution in social relations.

The use of punishment does not help in the education of children or the improvement of the social order. Enforcing punishment makes morality pointless. Punishment has been responsible for immeasurable misery. Mostly due to conditioning in childhood, people cannot see that to improve the human condition, it is necessary to repay good for evil, not evil for evil. Some day, perhaps centuries from now, our descendants will be amazed that we could have been so blind to the senselessness, cruelty, and harmfulness of returning evil for evil through trials, prisons, and capital punishment.

5. In personal relations, brotherly/sisterly love and not using violent means to resist evil must be substituted for retribution.

When someone strikes you on the right cheek, turn the left also—this is the Christian ideal. It does not matter who used force first; violence is always evil and always generates evil. The desire for vengeance is natural only to the animal in us, not to our reason. The thinking person understands the teaching of love, which allows no violence; only love conquers evil. We should not try to justify punishments with theories because at the root of these theories are wrong views. On the contrary, we need but forgive and return good for evil. Forgiveness has no limits.

6. Not using violent means to resist evil is as essential in social as in personal relations.

It is wrong to think that the present order of things would be disrupted if we were to cease threatening evil with punishment. On the contrary, real life would begin. The appearance that evil has power over good is false and ungrounded; as a result of that false notion, many people feel that it is not only permitted, but even directly beneficial to treat others violently. Punishment is seen as natural because people view Christianity as not practical, not suited to "real life." Ordering the practical affairs of people is regarded as more important than dwelling in the "dream" of repaying evil with good. But the supposedly essential and practical problems of ordering life can be reduced to one question: is it reasonable or unreasonable to return evil for evil? This problem was definitely settled by the teachings of Jesus twenty centuries ago. We should not pretend that we do not know the problem or its solution.

7. The view that violence is necessary is beginning to be seen for what it is; an understanding of the true facts is sinking into the conscience of humanity.

In the past, punishment was accepted without question as a result of the uncritical acceptance, by the masses, of those in power. In fact, the masses then allowed themselves to be subjected to the rulers, whose authority was unchallenged. That relationship has been changing in our age. As a result, humankind is beginning to realize that we do not have the right to punish others. Punishment is a theory which humankind is beginning to outgrow. Has not the spirit of the Gospels penetrated into the conscience of nations? Are they not beginning to see the light? Do we not hear from all sides a call for more equitable laws, for protection of the weak by institutions based on the principles of justice and equality? We must hope that the old enmity between those who once were separated by force will gradually die out. Such feelings are opening a new path for the nations, the law of which will not be force but love.

CHAPTER SIXTEEN

Vanity

He had received this Order, which he greatly prized,
while serving in the Caucasus, because a number of
Russian peasants . . . had killed at his command
more than a thousand men . . . .
Later on he served in Poland, and there also made
Russian peasants commit many different crimes, and
got more Orders and decorations for his uniform.

from *Resurrection*

Nothing distorts life and robs us of true happiness as much as the habit of living, not according to wise teachings and our own conscience, but for the approval of those around us.

1. In what consists the temptation of vanity?

One of the greatest causes of evil in life is our deep-seated desire for the approval of others. More than any other temptation, this desire leads us away from the truly good life, because it turns us away from our true self, the self that is capable of attaining goodness. For the sake of this desire people sell their souls, as it were, because they replace their inner life with another imaginary life that they feel is acceptable to others, yet is wholly foreign to their true being. We steadily feed this other foreign life with the thoughts and attitudes at large in the world of people around us, in the hope that we will reflect these things back to others and thus gain a measure of solidarity or oneness with them. These ideas which we adopt are those of the great majority of people. Yet, since there are more foolish people in the world than there are wise people, we constantly reflect foolishness. In the meantime this imaginary person masks the true self from sight, and it is this self that has a conscience and can attain true happiness and the true meaning of life. This imaginary person covers up the truth, which is that only the approval of God matters.

2. The fact that many people are of one opinion does not prove that this opinion is correct.

Actions and beliefs of an evil nature are wrong even if many people follow them, and even boast about them. We must examine carefully those actions and beliefs, and not follow them just because most other people do so. When we see that the multitudes are heaping praise on a particular person or idea, or despising another, it would be wise to examine the objects of praise and of scorn to determine why the multitudes have judged them to be so. In so doing, we often learn that the things that are praised should most likely be avoided, while those that are scorned may be something of true value for the wise person. Only through the exercise of our conscience, which should be the judge in these matters, will we be able to see and understand these things. Our life is not harmed as much by evil-doers who would corrupt us as by the unthinking multitude who drag us along like a whirlpool.

3. The ruinous effects of vanity.

People become slaves when they let themselves drift into the habits of society for the sake of following fashion. Even the wise can fall prey to this because they may value the praise of others rather than the judgment of their own conscience. But this desire for the praise of others is injurious to the soul and leads to a multitude of evil deeds such as warfare, robbery and lies. Even study, when done for praise rather than for the sake of the spirit, becomes not only useless but makes people less wise than they were before they started. Only concern for the opinions of others can explain why people tell lies. They are afraid they will not be praised if they tell the truth and believe they will be praised if they tell a lie. People still live by many old customs in which they no longer believe because they think others would criticize them if they stopped believing in these customs.

4. Combatting the temptation of vanity.

We must ultimately free ourselves from the desire for the praise of others if we are to find not only true happiness, but our true worth. From the very beginning of life we live for the desires of the body (animal passions). As we become older, the opinion of others (vanity) is more important to us than bodily desires. When we become aware of the Spirit within us, we give up bodily desires, amusements, and the opinions of others in order to live for the needs of the spirit.

Those who have made self-perfecting the goal of their lives must be prepared for criticism. The most important thing for you to know is what you think of yourself. Everyone at some time is subject to ridicule, but we soon come to realize that this ridicule means nothing. Do not worry about the judgment (praise or criticism) of other people, but strive to preserve your spiritual life. Life was given you not for show, but for you to live. Many people, contrary to what their consciences tell them, continue yielding to animal passions. They do so because others are doing the same—and others are doing what they do for the same reason. The only way out of this is to free ourselves from dependence on the opinions of others. Be concerned not about what other people think of you, but about whether you are fulfilling your destiny before the higher power which sent you into the world.

5. Heed your soul, and not your reputation.

Pay attention to your soul, and not to your reputation. To try to convince people that we are good is much harder than to become what we would have people think us to be. If you worry about what people think, you will never decide upon anything, for some people approve of one thing, others of another. Submitting to others' approval and decisions is a humiliating form of slavery. It is necessary to listen to your conscience and decide for yourself. It is also much easier to do so. Do what you think is right, and do not be guided by the conflicting opinions of others. In order to live a better life, you must form new habits of your own without caring about what people consider good or evil. If you do a good deed for the sake of the higher values you believe in, you will not care if others do not know about it.

6. He who lives the true life does not require the praise of people.

Train yourself to live so as not to think of the opinion of others, but to live only for the fulfillment of the law of your life, the will of God. If you try to live according to God's will, you will have no desire to do good deeds for human praise. You can never know how to please people (who are continuously subject to new desires), but you *can* know how to please the Spirit within you.

This will give your soul a feeling of freedom, peace, stability, and such a certain knowledge that your path is true, as one who lives for human praise can never know. All of us can train ourselves to live like this.

Addendum on Vanity

When the whole world lives a life that is not right, we fail to notice it; but should one awaken spiritually and live a godly life, the evil lives of others become immediately apparent. And the others always persecute those who do not live like the rest.

SUPERSTITIONS

CHAPTER SEVENTEEN

The Superstition of Government (the State)

*The great masses of unlearned people are under the constant
and intense hypnotic influence of the government.*
from "Religion and Morality"

*. . . [he explained to his friends]
how they were all being deceived by the State,
and how they ought to disentangle themselves
from the deception they were in.*
from *Resurrection*

The superstition of government is its claim to be united with only the people of one nation and separated from the rest of the people in the world—those belonging to other nations. As a result of this false doctrine, people torment, murder, and rob people of other nations (in international wars) and of their own nation (in civil wars). We are freed from this false teaching when we realize that the same spirit is within everyone. Once we recognize this, we can no longer have faith in governments which separate what God has united.

1. The falsehood and deception in the doctrine of the state.

Even the most devoted rulers should not be obeyed without question. But many citizens blindly obey and even cringe before corrupt rulers who rob them and treat them cruelly. Why do millions of people without protest allow a handful of rulers to control their lives? This happens every day in every country: a few people lord it over hundreds of thousands of villages and deprive them of their freedom.

We do not need to overthrow these few individuals who oppress all others; all we need to do is not agree to our own slavery, the robbery of our fields and homes, and the taking of our children to fight in wars. There is no need to attack that enemy, the government. If we do not give it support it will fall apart and we will be free.

People betray themselves by surrendering their freedom, their conscience, and their very lives to the government. If we even wish to no longer serve corrupt rulers and be free, we *will* break free.

Currently the happiness of governments grows to the same extent as the unhappiness of their citizens. Governments deceive us when they say they are carrying out our

---

Editor's Note: In this chapter Tolstoy discusses the typical evils of government. In the context of this discussion, the chapter does not address the possibility of any humane model of government which would minimize those evils or abuses. Nor does Tolstoy clearly acknowledge here the necessity in large populations of some kind of government to avoid destructive anarchy and chaos. However, in other writings Tolstoy is less extreme and in effect acknowledges the need for some extent of government. In his day the choice seemed to him to be between abusive government and a spiritually motivated distrust of the abuses of government. Were he with us today, he would most certainly make another choice and endorse granting much more room to local and regional government—the path travelled by Gandhi and many of his followers.

wishes—while they seize the product of our labor, while they imprison people, condemn them to death, and use them to conduct war (mass murder). Freedom is not possible for those who identify narrowly with any one particular nation. The problem is the existence of *separate* states or governments. A false and unnecessary government cannot grant its citizens true freedom, as it pretends to do with monarchies, republics, and democracies. Governments are so powerful that they persuade even believers to go against their conscience and their faith while obeying the civil and military authorities who order them to rob and judge people, condemn them to death, and kill other human beings in war. In fact, governments train people to perform deeds that are contrary to God's law. Rulers, statesmen, and the wealthy convince themselves and others that we cannot live without government; but the poor, to whom the government gives nothing, support it because they believe in its false doctrine.

A question often asked is, "What would replace our civilization if the people, with their limited knowledge and reason, did away with the government?" Undistorted Christianity provides the answer to this falsehood by pointing out what is good and what is evil in the life of every person. The message provided by religions, "Do unto others as you would have them do unto you," is so simple, clear, and unquestionable that even a child can understand it, and no philosopher can prove it wrong.

2. The superstition of inequality, marking government officials as distinct from the entire remainder of a nation.

Under threat of punishment, people have become accustomed to being told what they may and may not do by "the authorities" (the state or government). If we ask, "*Who* are the authorities?" we learn that they are not special individuals but simply people, similar to everyone else. Ironically, their orders and policies are carried out by the same citizens who are oppressed by these orders. Now, the evils of government are greater than the evils which government is supposed to prevent. No one knows what would happen if there were no government, but we certainly know that without its coercive force people's lives would be better. Now the way people are ruled is more wicked than would be the case without government. Some government leaders are cruel, and fall below the moral standards of the times.

As was pointed out by a famous government expert, rulers need not be merciful, true to their word, philanthropic, religious, or honest, but merely give the *appearance* that they are; *actually* having such qualities could be damaging to them. Rulers often have to act against what their conscience, love of humankind, and religious faith tell them. They need to change their convictions according to the circumstances. Most citizens uncritically judge things by their appearance; therefore, they do not see through such false appearances as the mask of religious devotion or other masks worn by certain rulers. Most citizens fear to express an opinion contrary to that of the majority, and are afraid of offending the higher authorities.

While robbers take from the rich, governments take from the poor and help the rich in their crimes. They corrupt entire generations with false religious and patriotic doctrine. Not even the cruelest robbers could compare with the cruelty of governments that practice solitary confinement, capital punishment, and the sacrificing of many lives in wars. The major evil of government is not that it wastes so many lives, but that it represses love and fosters disunity among people.

3. Government is based on violence.

Government demands of its citizens force and support of force, and thus all citizens who willingly comply are their own oppressors. Every government arms a police force and an army so that they can carry out the government's will by force, including killing those whom the government wishes to kill. An army, which is nothing but a collection of trained and disciplined murderers, is always the foundation of authority and political power. The first duty of an army is to support the governmental power and get rid of the government's rivals. Building up armies and weapons has always been the job of the military. War is an outcome of existing military buildup, and the immediate reason for it is usually a dispute between governments for authority. Besides driving off outside enemies, one important duty of the army is to protect the government against oppressed and enslaved citizens.

Humans are so foolish that they allow themselves to be sent to fight wars, like cattle driven to the slaughterhouse, as if the life of each person were not his own property. If thinking people knew how to cooperate, they would dispel the myth that nations, borders and flags are more important than the awareness of our being a single human family. But those bureaucratic freeloaders in every government whose jobs depend on war prevent thinking people from getting organized and refusing to participate in their mutual murder. It is absurd that two persons from opposite sides of a river should kill each other because their rulers have a dispute.

Some people condemn wars and other uses of violence, yet in practice promote violence because of the kind of work they do. Thus, those who work in an arms factory are participating in preparations for murder. Similarly, a tax-collector who takes money from the poor participates in government-sponsored violence.

War drains a nation's economy. Much of the income of government goes toward the interest on debts incurred in wartime and toward maintaining their armies. This is criminal, for the greatest crimes are not occasional acts of violence, but are those committed continually, without being acknowledged as crimes.

4. Government was a temporary form of life in society.

Perhaps government was once a necessary arrangement, but now people must try to introduce a system in which violence is unnecessary and impossible. Inner self-perfecting (which does not allow violence) helps us implement such a system. Just as we undergo changes as we move through periods in life, humanity as a whole changes as it moves from youth onto maturity. We must now make the transition from the animal to the human stage, which is possible only with the abolition of government. People are already beginning to understand that government is an institution whose time is over; and it is now maintained only through falsity. In due time, guns will be museum pieces—as obsolete as government itself already is.

5. Laws do not reform and improve, but instead worsen and corrupt people.

Government creates criminals faster than it can punish them, first by establishing numerous laws which give rise to crimes, and then by creating even more laws to punish those who commit the crimes. Laws never make people more just. Government makes as many laws as there are relationships among people, and as a result there are countless laws, decrees, and edicts. As an example, laws in France number well over 50,000.

If we look at the situation of those living under any government (tyrannical or democratic), we see how much slavery they endure, imagining they are free. Innumerable laws regulate every possible aspect of our lives: marriage, divorce, how to behave to one's children, immunization and schooling of those children, inheritance, how to relate to one's employees, specifications for houses people want to build. We must devote a large portion of our labor to pay the interest on debts incurred in the times of our grandparents, and we must pay every time we receive an inheritance or buy or occupy land.

In addition, most governments order their young men into military slavery. Not realizing they are slaves, such enlisted soldiers are often proud to be citizens of their "great" governments, just as servants are proud of the importance of their masters. People are all equal by nature, and all have an ability to reason; yet some govern others and force them to live a certain way. This should not be. People need only obey the spirit within themselves—their conscience. There is a duty for us to obey our conscience whenever it is in conflict with rulers, congresses, senates, or lawcourts. When we compare our society with traditional native American communities, we see that the most evil is found where there are most laws.

6. Justification for the necessity of the governmental apparatus.

You are responsible for your support of the government. Even if you do not see those whom you torment and kill, you are still a tormentor or a murderer. It is said that a government is fair and just because it is established by the majority of votes, but that is not true because governmental structures are established not by votes but by strength. One person has no right to have control over the many, and the many do not have the right to control one person. When 51% decide the fate of 49%, this is not much better than rule by the few (10% controlling the fate of 90%). Existing governments are in no way equipped to help us move toward a society governed by the desire for justice. Government has not always existed, and if it exists now, that does not prove that it must always exist.

7. Christians should not take part in affairs of government.

Governments, like churches, are treated with reverence until we understand that they are only a deception, and then we can only feel aversion toward them. When the government's demands go against one's conscience, a true person of principles should take a stand and not obey such demands. If we choose to obey the authorities instead of God, it is like obeying not the master of the house one lives in, but the first person one meets in the street. If people were not drugged by the false teachings of the government, they would ask to be left in peace, rather than perform the evil deeds the government commands, such as killing in wars.

The teachings of Jesus and of the world have always been and will be contradictory, as Jesus taught that no one should kill or use violence against another, whereas governments force some people to punish or kill others (such as through the death penalty or in war). According to Jesus a person should never kill, nor do violence to friend or foe. Jesus knew that those who followed his teaching would be tormented, killed, and hated as he was.

Anarchists, who rightfully believe that nothing is worse

than the current violence of the authorities, are mistaken in thinking that revolution can lead to anarchy, for anarchy will come only when more and more people no longer need the protection of governmental authority. Anarchy does not mean the absence of institutions, but only the absence of those institutions which use violence to force people to submit.

A true Christian cannot be a member of a society that has an army and military institutions, and which sends its soldiers to kill their own foreign brothers or commit murder or violence in the name of God. My authorization is the necessary condition for my government to commit such horrors, and the only moral step I can take is to withdraw such authorization.

CHAPTER EIGHTEEN

False Religious Practice

The [church] service began. The priest, having dressed
himself up in a strange and very inconvenient garb of
gold cloth . . . [was] repeating at the same time
different names and prayers. Meanwhile the deacon
first read prayers [in the ancient Slavonic Church
language], difficult to understand in themselves
and rendered still more incomprehensible
by being read very fast . . .

from *Resurrection*

False religious practices are those which are harmful rather than helpful. Many people follow them as a result of faith in certain religious leaders who advocate such practices.

1. The deceit of false religious practice.

Many people follow religious teachings because everyone else follows them, and not because of any spiritual need. Because people live lives full of faults and failings they adapt their religion to suit their lives in order to relieve their conscience. In so doing, people are lying to themselves. If we accept without reasoning false religious teachings which we should examine by the light of our reason, we lose the capacity to reason. Our freedom consists in learning to think with our own minds. However, following false religious teachings means taking on faith three kinds of false beliefs:

a) the belief that it is possible to learn by experience that which does not make sense according to laws of experience—or, *belief in miracles;*

b) admitting as a basis for our moral self-improvement beliefs which we cannot grasp by our reason—or, *belief in mysteries;*

c) the belief that we can, by mysterious and supernatural means, induce God to influence our moral behavior—or, *belief in grace.*

2. False religious beliefs meet the lowest—not the highest—need of the human spirit.

True religion contains nothing but laws which can hold up to our reasoning. We can please God by good living, and in no other way. When praying to God we must not ask for material and worldly things (such as rain, recovery from illness, or delivery from enemies). Rather, when praying we should isolate ourselves and reexamine our life, our weaknesses, actions, and feelings, not in the light of demands of outward circumstances, but in the light of the spirit of which we are conscious. And we should ask for guidance.

3. Outward rituals observed by the churches.

False religious practices follow arbitrary rules which have

nothing to do with self-improvement and better living. True religion is based on the constant striving for a better way of living and serving the Supreme Being. People who perform acts which have no real good in them in order to gain God's favor and to gain material results are practicing fetishism (assigning special magical power to an object). When praying, one must pray in secret because when you pray in public you are concerned about what people will think, rather than heeding your spirit.

4. Multiplicity of church teachings and the one true religion.

One must not accept one's faith simply because one was born into it, and one must not reject others' beliefs simply because they are not one's own. Your faith will not become truth just because you declare to yourself and to others that it is the one true faith.

5. Effects of professing false religions.

In the past, bodies such as the Catholic and Anglican Churches have used the most ruthless means of maintaining their religion and dealing with those who preach against them. (Examples are the torture and execution of Dr. Leighton by Anglicans in 1682, and the burning of Johannes Hus at the stake by Catholics in 1415.) But the most cruel method of spreading false doctrines is planting them in the minds of children, even when the adults may not believe them, but merely pay lip-service to them. Humans never commit evil deeds with greater confidence and assurance of being right than when committing these deeds in the name of false religion.

6. What is true religion?

We are all brothers and sisters, and contain within us goodness. Therefore we should not place others higher than ourselves because they may mislead us. True religion is based on our love for one another and love for God, and it focuses on how we should act—treat others as you would have them treat you. Follow the simple truth of love and refuse to follow all that is false. We become happy only when we serve others and not our own selves. True religion is based on the constant striving to achieve this level of love, whereas dismissing this as an impossible goal and altering the teachings of Jesus into another practice is falsehood. We must not fall into the trap of thinking our faith is better than anyone else's, because all humans have an inner light and are striving to reach perfection.

7. The true single faith unites humans more and more.

Truth cannot be extinguished but it can be developed. Just as each person must change, so humanity as a whole must pass from lower to higher stages of development. From the beginning of humankind, people have had to suffer for the sake of bringing new truths to light. Do not lose faith that eventually truth shall unite us all.

CHAPTER NINETEEN

False Science

*. . . there is a whole series of most diffused sciences
which try to reply to irrelevant questions.
Semi-sciences of that kind [are] the juridical
and the social-historical [sciences] . . .*

from *A Confession*

The superstition of science (blind belief in science) is the belief that the only true knowledge needed for all people's lives is found in the small part of information selected on a random basis by a small group of researchers from the limitless knowledge available. These scientists have set themselves apart from the obligation to labor which is absolutely necessary for life and, for that reason, live an unprincipled high social life without aiding real human labor.

1. What is the superstition of science about?

Accepting as truth that which is offered by academics and scientists, without stopping to examine it by the exercise of our reason, is the superstition of science. Just as there are false teachings of religion, there are also false teachings of science. What today is called science is not what is necessary to all people, but what is determined by scientists—a small group who have taken upon themselves the right to determine what is true science. Today scientists are as blindly believed as priests were in ages past. Because they use unclear language and make simple things hard to understand, they are often accepted without question. The truly wise person uses plain and simple language to express thoughts so that all will understand.

2. False science serves as a justification for the present social order.

The useful purpose of science is the discovery of truths helpful to humankind. However, scientists say that all their work is useful. In contrast to true science, misguided science justifies harmful deceptions. Deceptive science, like deceptive religion, comes from the desire to justify one's weaknesses. Understanding that their life is wrong, people should try hard to change their behavior, and lead a better life. But sciences such as economics, religious studies, law, criminology, science of police administration, political science, history, sociology, and philosophy interfere. These sciences say that people are not to blame for their evil lives and need not try to discontinue their evil actions in order to live better. These sciences merely come up with laws that provide a description and justification of indifferent or evil behavior. These misguided sciences "prove" that evil people function in accordance with "laws" and need not change their behavior. This fraud is most unreasonable and contrary to our conscience.

We dimly recognize the falsity of our social order, but do not subject it to rational examination. For we believe that humans, who have always accepted compulsory social order, religion, and science, cannot live without them.

If money is needed in order to become more learned, if learning is bought and sold, both the buyer and the seller deceive themselves. The profiteers of science should be driven from their academic strongholds.

3. The harmful effects of the superstition of science.

The development of false science is accompanied by a corruption of morals. Much of modern science, spreading harmful beliefs (such as that life is solely a product of material forces), deserves only contempt and ridicule. The cause of our unfortunate social conditions is that our youths are taught useless and utter nonsense rather than the meaning of life and how to live. All of this futile knowledge serves to maintain the existing order and to profit the scientists, but brings only more uncertainty, hatred, and enmity to the rest of us. We cannot study everything, and without focused values we study only those things which please scientists.

4. Areas of study are numberless, comprehension is limited.

Philosophy and astronomy have taught us the extent of our ignorance. We learn very little and deceive ourselves about the rest. We cannot know the part without knowing the whole. To try is folly. It is the quality of knowledge that is important, and not the quantity. Study your soul, train your mind to be cautious in judgment, instill mercy in your self. Learn to know people and arm yourself with courage to speak the truth for the good of all. One can know many things without knowing that which is necessary. God is in all things, so narrow study may have some value if the goal is to know human nature. Use what you learn to speak for the good of humankind. The ability to learn is limited: there are so many problems to solve that we should not waste our lives on mere words that take away from our understanding of life and harm the truth. Science is food for the mind, and it may be harmful just as some food is harmful to the body. It is possible to overeat mentally and be made sick thereby. Take mental food only when knowledge is important for the spirit.

5. Knowledge is limitless. The aim of true science is to select the most important and needed information.

It is shameful to pretend to know more than one does; but it is not shameful to have limited knowledge. We burden ourselves with useless facts and ideas. We need not know everything, but must know the meaning of our life. The study of what is useless mental rubbish weakens the mind and actually hinders our learning what is important. Self-deception and mental clutter often accompany superficial knowledge, while even the greatest scientist remains just as ignorant in some areas as the uneducated person. Much knowledge does not always make a person wise. The main thing is to know what is most important out of the whole range of possible knowledge. That is understood by all. Simple people, not learned enough to reason wrongly, can have this higher knowledge without intellectual pride. The pursuit of knowledge for its own sake leads to spiritual death. Do not fear lack of knowledge, but fear too much knowledge, especially if it is for profit or praise. The most important things to know are how we should live in the world and what we should do; such knowledge leads to greater wisdom than having answers for numerous complex but trivial questions.

6. The substance and purpose of true science

True science, which is understood by all, is conducted for the good of humankind, not for profit. The only good (true) science is that which helps us to improve ourselves. The deceit of false science is harmful and must be fought by means of the truth. The wise among all nations have taught that which is most necessary to know. Such wise people are able to know what a person's purpose and fulfillment are about. Only one who knows this can judge the importance of all other kinds of knowledge. True science deals with real life—it teaches us how to live and what to do. False science is unable to solve the direct and simple questions of life. Wisdom can reveal truths which scientific investigation cannot. To practice false science is to indulge in empty occupations that keep us away from the true tasks of life. Do not waste time on unnecessary studies. Rather, work on improving yourself.

7. On reading books.

Be selective in your reading. You cannot read all books; only those written by the best authors of all ages and nations teach us what is most important. Bad books do nothing but lighten your wallet and clutter your mind. Such books are not only useless, but harmful. It is better never to read a book than to read many books and to believe everything that is contained in them. In order to live justly and well we must seek out the truths set forth by the wise and holy ones who have preceded us. Blind belief can be overcome by the study of humankind's past actions toward the recognition and expression of the common eternal truth.

8. Of independent thinking.

We should make use of the knowledge of humankind, but everything should be examined by our reason; what we realize by ourselves is deeper knowledge. We must learn to think for ourselves and make our own decisions about what we learn. A natural mind (one that thinks independently) may replace almost any amount of learning, but no amount of learning can replace a natural mind. Too much reading is harmful to thinking. The greatest thinkers do the least reading. If we teach *how* to think, then rote learning and dead knowledge are not needed. People should be taught how to think and not merely that they should think.

POSITIVE APPROACHES AND PRACTICES

CHAPTER TWENTY

Effort

*Plato's virtues, beginning with self-control,
advanced through courage and wisdom
to justice . . .*

Faults, temptations, and superstitions block the soul and hide it from our awareness. In order to reveal our soul, we must make an effort of consciousness, and therefore this effort is the main task of our life.

1. Deliverance from faults, temptations, and superstitions is in effort.

Only by efforts of our consciousness can we be delivered from faults, temptations, and superstitions which deprive us of happiness and delay the coming of the Kingdom of God. To become even better is the whole concern of life, and one can become better only by effort. In the material world we achieve nothing without effort; so also in the life of the soul. True strength is not muscle, money, or power, but rather mastery over self. Every effort, no matter how difficult to reach or how unimportant the goal, strengthens the soul. All that is good and beneficial to us requires an effort; evil deeds, the source of our misfortune, are easy to perform. Truth does manifest itself to us, but we fail to see it. Truth wants us to seek truth.

2. Living for the soul requires effort.

I am an instrument with which God performs his work. I can share in the work of God by keeping my spirit in good order, sharp and aware. The most precious thing for us is to be free to live according to our own will and not to that of another person. Our life is a gradual passing from the lower animal nature to an ever increasing consciousness of our spiritual life. If I live for the spirit within, I will be free. In order to live for the spirit I must subdue the passions of the body. We make an effort to awaken when a dream becomes so horrible that we cannot bear it. Even so, when life becomes unbearable, we must make mental efforts to awaken a new, superior spiritual life. If we do not make efforts to overcome faults, temptations, and superstitions, our body soon attains mastery over us. The work of daily growth in spirit and in love is the only true work, and all other work is useful only as long as this chief work of life is performed. A bad life can be and must be corrected not through external changes, but through a change within, a change in the spirit. This is the only important life work for all people. Take a silkworm for a pattern. It toils until it has strength to fly. You are clinging to earth. Toil over your spirit and you will receive wings.

3. Perfecting of self is attained only by an effort of consciousness.

Faults cannot be overcome all at once. There is only one way to grow better: by wise judgment and constant patient effort. The joy of goodness and truth is in the efforts made to attain it. Those who follow the rule of constant effort shall attain what they seek. Your business is not in attaining perfection, it is in the constant striving after it. Do not think lightly of the good or evil in your heart: even as drops will fill a vessel with water, little by little you will be filled with good or evil. Perform good deeds, and you will be filled with good. In order to be good, you must not commit a single unkind action without reproving yourself. And if you become accustomed to kindness, joy will ever reign in your heart. The merit of a person, however, is not measured by outstanding feats, but by his daily effort.

4. In striving after perfection we must rely on our own strength alone.

It is a mistake to ask God or even other people to rescue us out of an undesirable condition. If we make an effort of consciousness we can free ourselves. Our condition can change or improve only to the extent that we free ourselves from faults, temptations, and superstitions. Nothing weakens us more than seeking help outside our own efforts. If you have misdirected the course of your life, you must not think that divine intervention will set everything right. Within us is the knowledge of perfection. Within us also are obstacles to its attainment. Our condition is what we must work over in order to approach perfection. We are evil or pure in our own selves—another cannot save us. Some say we are born selfish, covetous, and lustful; that we cannot be otherwise. Yes, we can! We must develop our good inclinations. To make ourselves better is the principal task of life.

5. There is only one way to improve life in society— by the individual effort of people striving after a righteous and moral life.

In striving to live a righteous life people may draw nearer to the Kingdom of God. To improve the social order, all people must become better. The only thing you can do to improve society is to become better yourself. You might say that improvements in human life are brought about by the joint action of the whole society and not by individual effort. It is true that one swallow does not make springtime. But that does not mean that one swallow which senses springtime should refrain from flying, sit still, and wait. If every bud, every blade of grass did so, spring would never come. Christianity has failed to alter the social order of life because people await a change from external conditions and refuse to comprehend that this change is attained by the efforts of each individual. Life is evil because there are evil people. Therefore, in order to change life, we must become good by our own efforts. We cannot change others—they must change themselves. But we can change ourselves, and transform ourselves from evil people into good people. If we all begin to correct ourselves, then immediately all lives will improve. It is our fault that life is evil, and only we can make it good.

6. The effort of striving after perfection yields true happiness.

The reward of goodness is in the very effort of a good action. For beginners, spiritual work is not easy; it is even at times painful. So, do not look for quick results. Such mental effort is not a means for attaining a blessing, but this effort in itself is a blessing. The highest wisdom of humanity was not born within us; we must labor to attain it and the greater our labor, the greater our reward. All false arguments that fate controls all things will never silence the two faithful witnesses of freedom: the pangs of conscience and the value of suffering. All those who have chosen the path of evil hear in the depths of their heart the disapproving voice that gives them no rest, and that constantly asks: "Why did you turn from the path of goodness? You could, and still can, make an effort. You are a free agent. It is within your power to remain imprisoned by faults or to free yourself from them."

CHAPTER TWENTY-ONE

Living in the Present

*Remember . . . : There is only one time
that is important—Now!
It is the most important time
because it is the only time
when we have any power.*

from "Three Questions"

People imagine that their life is in the past or in the future. This is wrong: the true life always *is* in that timeless spot, where the past and the future meet, and which we inexactly call the present. Only in this timeless point of the present are we free, and therefore our true life is in the present alone.

1. The true life is in the present.

Since the past is no more, and the future has not yet come, only that point where they meet is the whole of our life. We only imagine that there is time. There is neither time nor space: both are necessary to us only for the understanding of things. Life seems to be in time and space, because only in time and space can there be motion, that is, striving toward expansion, illumination, and perfection. If there were no time and space, there would be no motion and therefore no life. There is only an instant which is our whole life, and all our strength must be invested in this one instant.

2. The spiritual life of humans is outside time and space.

Time exists for the body (the physical life) alone, but our spiritual being is always beyond time, because the activity of the spirit is only in the effort of the mind. And the effort of the mind is always beyond time, for it is always in the present and the present is not in time. It is well to remember frequently that our true life is not the outward physical life, but an inner and spiritual life which has no beginning and no end.

3. True life is only in the present.

We are able to remember the past and to imagine the future only to help us better decide our actions in the present. We are tormented by our past and spoil our future only because we pay little attention to the present. The past is gone, the future is not yet, only the present exists. We must train ourselves to remember that nothing is important except what we are doing right now. All else is a dream. Living the present moment in the spirit is all that matters. A wise man once said: "The most important thing is to love all people; the most important person is the one you are with right now, and the most important time is the present."

4. Love is manifested in the present only.

Loving others is the most important thing in life. You cannot love in the past or future. You can love only in the present, *now*, this instant. To love means to do good. Love is that which we do for the good of others. If you can do a good deed or show love to someone, do it at once, otherwise the chance may pass, never to return. We cannot love in the future, for there is no future; there is only the present. God dwells within us right now and therefore the present moment is the most important moment. Make use of all the forces of your soul so that this moment will not pass in vain.

5. The temptation of preparing for life instead of living it.

To think that we will live a better and more loving life some time in the future is a mistake because the future does not belong to us. We must lead the best life that we can right now, just as we are. Yet children, adults, and older people keep making many plans for the future, without knowing whether they will survive until evening. Love is the only improvement we can make and that is made only in the present. Death can interfere with future plans, but it cannot keep us from fulfilling the will of God (to love all people) at this moment of our life. Nothing outside us—family, poverty, illness, or prison—can keep us from this. We can change thoughts of fear and hate to thoughts of love. Every moment of our life is our chance to use our will to undertake the best action we can; no one can take this away from us. Each moment is the best because it is the only one we have. Do not waste energy wishing your life were different, that you had other possessions or circumstances. In the spiritual life, nothing is better than what is.

6. The consequences of our acts are God's business, not ours.

We can never know all the consequences of our acts. The genuinely good life occurs when we have no concern for what will happen to our bodies, but for what we now need for our souls—to be in union with all people and with God. When we live in harmony with God, we need not give thought to the consequences of our acts. The reward of a good life is not in the future, but is in the present. Do well in the present, and have no other concern.

7. For those who realize the meaning of life in the present, life after death is not a real issue.

Excessive thinking about a future life only confuses us. *Life* and *future* are contradictory terms; life can be in the present only. We must honestly and carefully perform the task set before us, no matter what our fate will be after death. The main problem of our life is whether, in the brief span of life granted us, we do the will of God who sent us here. In the course of a good life, the importance of time and the interest in life after death gradually fade away. The older we become the more quickly time passes, and the less importance is attached to what will be, but increasingly more to that which *is*.

CHAPTER TWENTY-TWO

Non-Acting

Follow this advice: look around oneself,
think about the result of one's work
or occupation, and ask oneself: What am I?
Why do I live? [We] need only pause
in what we are now doing.

from "Non-Acting"

People spoil their lives not so much by failing to do what they should do as by doing that which they should not do. Therefore the greatest effort we need for a good life is to stop doing that which we should not do.

1. Above all else, a good life requires refraining from wrong acting.

The most important task for all people is to live a good life. This means not so much to do the good things we can do, as to stop doing the wrong or evil things we can leave undone. All people know our present life is evil and they not only condemn it, but try doing all kinds of imaginative and difficult things which they think will make it better. But instead of improving, life becomes worse. This is because people do not stop doing those things which make our life bad. We can only know what we *should* do when we understand what we *should not* do. If we stop doing what we should not do, we will certainly do the things we should do. If you are not sure whether to do or not to do something, it is always better not to do it. If you are sure it is the right thing to do, you will not question it. If you question its value at all, you should stop it right away, for you may be sure that it is not entirely good. For one occasion when you will regret not having done a good action, there will be hundreds of times when you will regret doing a bad action that you should not have done. If you want to do something so much you feel you cannot stop yourself, do not trust yourself. You *can* stop if you convince yourself ahead of time that you can. Stopping is within our reach. We can always stop. It is useful for us to review our past deeds and ponder on them so as to learn when not to act.

2. Consequences of not refraining from action.

Less harm results from not doing what we should do than from doing what we should not do. Not stopping from doing one action weakens our power to stop another. The more difficult a situation seems to be, the less action it calls for. Actions often spoil what is becoming better. Most people who are considered mean have become so by accepting their bad moods and not making an effort to stop themselves. If you feel you do not have the strength to stop yourself from following a physical desire, it is because you didn't stop when you could have stopped, and the desire has become a habit.

3. Not all activity is worthy of respect.

Not all activity is worthwhile. It is important to question our activities, pursue those which are good, and stop those which are harmful. Often we stop necessary and important activities in order to continue mindless and harmful ones. It would be better to do nothing than to do that which is unnecessary and harmful.

We should carefully examine various kinds of "activity." One person works day after day as a judge, condemning people to various sentences; another is busy teaching soldiers to shoot and kill; a third is a money lender. While involved in such "occupations," these people all lead lives of plenty (luxury) made possible by what is supplied to them by the labor of others. Much of such would-be important "business," which seems so necessary to many people could, with no loss to humankind, be left undone and be replaced by meaningful activity (including play). On the other hand, overly busy activity is not needed and is even harmful.

4. Human beings can only restrain themselves from wrong actions when they realize that they are spiritual and not physical beings.

When we realize that we are spiritual beings instead of physical beings we no longer need to do what our bodies desire; instead, our bodies will do what our souls desire. This will teach us to keep from doing what is harmful. When the spirit is asleep and inactive (when we do not listen to God within us), we do what people around us do. Do not yield to outside influences which go against your conscience and lead to wrong actions. Only if from childhood you have trained the body to obey the soul is it easy to stop doing what you should not do. Those who do not listen to the desires that go against the spirit will find life joyful and easy.

5. The more you combat unrestraint, the easier the struggle becomes.

In order to respect others, and to do to them as you want them to do to you, you must be in control of yourself. There is a struggle between our soul (reason) and our body desires (passions). This struggle is necessary: it is life. In order to be kind to others, we must train ourselves. Every time we greatly desire to do anything, we should stop and think whether it is truly good. It is important not to do evil acts, but it is also important to stop evil talk and evil thoughts. If you are part of a conversation which is becoming unkind or harmful to another, stop it and be silent. Try to say something kind instead. Do the same when wrong thoughts enter your head: stop, and try to think of something else. Do not give up this struggle. Even if you fail sometimes, each effort will make it easier to control your passions. In the beginning desire is like a beggar, then a guest, and then an owner of the house; do not open your heart to this beggar.

6. The value to individuals and the human race of refraining from harmful or wrong acting.

If you want to be free, learn to control your desires. According to the *Talmud*, one is wise who learns a little from everybody; one is rich who is content with his lot; one is strong who controls himself. Only the strong can boldly face evil and withstand it. Because Christianity calls not for action, but mostly for not acting, it has been labeled a teaching for the weak and meek. Yet, among the followers of this teaching thousands died a heroic death; they were the only people who courageously rose against evil. More strength is required to stop doing evil than to perform the most difficult act which we consider good. True strength is not in one who overcomes others but in one who overcomes self, not allowing the animal nature to govern one's soul. Only then is one free. True strength is in self-mastery. The Buddha points out that yielding to cravings will bind us in chains. Denying oneself, or postponing fulfillment of desires, gives a better capacity of enjoyment. Do not strive so much to do good as to *be* good. Cease doing all the unnecessary things that people are doing. Ninety-nine percent of our activities are not necessary. The effort needed to enter a new form of life is the effort not to follow the mainstream—the effort *not* to do those things which are not in harmony with our conscience.

CHAPTER TWENTY-THREE

Speech

Was it possible that all these words about justice,
law, religion, and God, and so on, were mere words,
veiling the coarsest cupidity and cruelty?
from *Resurrection*

The fact that the business of hearing men swear
on the Gospels, in which all oaths are distinctly forbidden, is
a bad occupation, never occurred to [the old priest].
from *Resurrection*

The third law [Matthew, Chapter 5] is that
man should never bind himself by oath.
from *Resurrection*

Words are expressions of thoughts, and can be used to unite people or to divide them; therefore they must be handled carefully.

1. Our speech is of utmost importance.

Our words are good or evil and can serve love or hatred, according to whether our thoughts are kind or harmful to others. If we are conscious that our thinking is the working of the Spirit within us, we will never let our words express thoughts that are harmful to others. Be careful what you say. Time passes, but the spoken word remains. Think before you speak and stop before you speak too much. After you have a lengthy conversation, check to see if what you said was unimportant or even harmful. Learn to ask intelligent questions, listen attentively, but say little. When asked a question answer briefly. Do not be ashamed to say, "I do not know." Stop talking when you have nothing more to say. Do not boast about yourself, judge others, or argue. Exaggerated praise is a form of lying. If we all said nothing harmful about anyone, much sorrow would be removed from the world. Say only good things or say nothing at all. However, do not remain silent when the situation calls for speaking up.

2. When you are angry, hold your tongue.

If you know how people should live and wish to help them, tell them your thoughts calmly and with kindness, never with irritation or anger. Do not speak if you are angry. Be silent until you are calm. In an argument, persuade with gentleness; try not to make the other person angry. In a dispute, try not to antagonize, but to persuade. Use firm arguments, but soft words. Defend the truth, not your own viewpoint.

3. Do not quarrel.

A quarrel is like water bursting through a dam; once it has broken through, there is no stopping it. Quarrels persuade no one, but divide people, create bitterness, and simply strengthen originally held positions; the truth is forgotten in them. A smart person puts an end to a quarrel. You may listen to quarrels, but do not participate. Do not be quick-tempered. The best answer to an insult is silence.

4. Do not judge.

Do not judge, so you are not judged. The standard you use to judge others will be applied to you, so do not pretend to be what you are not. Usually the faults we dislike most in others are those we have ourselves. Look for your own faults before you search for the faults of others. Remember that no one knows what is inside another's heart, nor all the circumstances of another's life, so do not judge. If you realize you are condemning someone, stop immediately. To condemn people to their face is harmful, and to condemn them behind their back is dishonest because it deceives them. Never trust a person who speaks badly about others and well about you. Avoid jokes at someone's expense, as well as backbiting. Do not gossip about others in order to be popular.

5. Harmful effects of unrestraint in words.

Words must be handled as carefully as a loaded gun. We condemn crimes of action (hitting someone, adultery, murder), but treat verbal crimes (censure, insult, gossip) lightly, yet they often do far worse damage. Just one foolish word can bring great harm, but the process may be gradual and unnoticeable. Idle talk promotes idleness; elimination of idle talk leads to elimination of idleness. Gossip harms three parties: the person being spoken about, the people being spoken to, and, above all, the speaker himself. Gossiping behind someone's back is especially harmful because it cannot serve as constructive criticism that brings about positive changes. The more you want to talk, the greater the danger that you will say something negative and harmful. Great is the strength of one who is silent even when right.

6. The value of silence.

Silence is often the best answer. Think before you speak. Speak only if what you have to say is better than silence. According to the *Talmud*, silence is the best kind of speech. He who speaks much ends up doing some wrong action. One useful rule of thumb in conversation is not to mention others' faults. When you want to speak, first stop and think about whom you want to benefit, yourself or others. If yourself, keep silent.

7. The value of restraint in words

The less you talk, the more work you'll get done. If you train yourself not to judge, you'll discover a greater capacity for love and life. Do not respond to insults with insults, but with silence. Focus on people's good points, not their shortcomings, and you will earn the love of others, which is the greatest good in life.

CHAPTER TWENTY-FOUR

Thought

He had committed no evil action,
but, what was far worse than an evil action,
he had entertained evil thoughts,
whence evil actions proceed.

from *Resurrection*

Even as we can stop doing an act which we know is wrong, so can we stop thinking a thought which we know is wrong. Because all acts begin in thoughts, to stop thinking thoughts that are harmful is a source of strength.

1. The purpose of thought.

You cannot free yourself from faults, temptations, and superstitions by physical effort, but only by effort of thought. Only when we strive in our thoughts to be unselfish, humble, and truthful will we have the strength to free ourselves. Thought points out to us that which hinders love. Nothing is more important than this effort to think right that summons conscience (the spirit within us). This voice of conscience may be summoned at all times from within by an effort of thought. Conscience gives us the wisdom to live right.

We are given the power to think so we can calmly bear misfortunes. Our reason tells us that all misfortunes pass away and are often turned into blessings; also that they work to our benefit. Yet people, instead of facing misfortunes, boldly try to avoid them. We can rejoice that we have the power not to grieve over what occurs outside our will, but to be grateful that our thoughts give us the power to turn misfortunes into blessings. All truth is already within the soul of everyone. If we do not choke it with falsehood, sooner or later it will reveal itself to us.

2. Human life is determined by a person's thoughts.

In order to change the way we feel or act we must first change our thoughts. To improve our life, we must first think and consider what is wrong with it before we can change it. It would be nice if wisdom could flow from a person who has much into another who has little; but in order to be able to learn from the wisdom of another, we must first think for ourselves. In order to learn how to live right, we must first teach ourselves how to think right. The changes in our life are determined not by visible acts such as marriage, change of work or location, but by the thoughts which come to us as we walk or eat, or in the middle of the night. If these thoughts tell us we acted wrongly in the past and should have acted differently, all our future acts, like slaves, serve these thoughts and obey their will. Our desires will not become good until we correct our habits of thought. Our thoughts, good or evil, send us to heaven or hell—not in the sky or underground, but right here in this life.

Similarly, the life of communities and nations is determined, not by events occurring among them, but by the thoughts which unite the majority of people within them. Wisdom is necessary to all people, and therefore everyone *can* be wise. Wisdom is knowing what is important in life and how to perform it. In order to know this, only one thing is necessary: remember that thought is a great thing, and therefore think. Thought is important because it determines our actions.

3. The main reason for human disasters is not people's actions but their thoughts.

Misfortunes are not due to what we have done, but to what we have thought. If we cannot keep from doing something wrong, it is because we first allowed ourselves to think about it without stopping our thoughts. Strive not to think about things that you believe are wrong or evil. More harmful than wrong or evil acts are those thoughts which lead to wrong acts. A wrong act need not be repeated, and one can be sorry for it. But wrong thoughts give birth to wrong acts. If you do not reject wrong thoughts and cherish good thoughts, you cannot avoid wrong acts. Good acts come from good thoughts only. Cherish good thoughts, searching for them in books of wisdom, in sensible conversations, and above all within yourself.

4. People have power over their thoughts.

It is possible to direct our thoughts. Therefore, in order to live a good life, we must work on our thoughts and not yield to wrong thoughts. Guard your thoughts, guard your words, guard your actions from being wrong: such is the program proposed by the Buddha. We cannot stop birds from flying over us, but we can keep them from building a nest on our heads. Similarly, we cannot stop wrong thoughts from flashing through our minds, but we can refuse to yield to them. If I want to benefit from my thoughts, I must try to think independently of my feelings or condition, without twisting my thoughts to justify the feelings I experience or the acts I commit. If I am tempted to judge another person, I can remember that judging is wrong and I myself have weaknesses. I should keep from judging even in my thoughts.

5. Live the spiritual life in order to have strength to rule your thoughts.

Our life improves or becomes worse depending upon whether we think of ourselves as spiritual or physical. Therefore, in order to change our condition, we must work on changing our thoughts. We can change our consciousness of physical being to consciousness of spiritual being by an effort of thought. True power to change our life and the life of all people comes from the spirit. If we think of ourselves as physical beings, we weaken our true life and strengthen desires (passions), conflicts, greed, hatred, and fear of death. If we think of ourselves as spiritual beings, we strengthen our true life, release love, and free ourselves from those things which harm us. When you are in doubt about what is good or evil, withdraw from the world, listen to the spirit within and all doubt will vanish. Worrying about the judgment of the world prevents you from seeing what is good or evil.

6. The opportunity of communing in thought with the living and the dead is one of our choicest blessings.

The efforts that deliver people from faults, temptations, and superstitions have their beginning in thoughts. The principal aid to this struggle is the ability to commune with the reasoning activity of the sages and saints who have come before us. Such communion—repetition of those words wherein these individuals expressed their relation to their soul, to other people, and to the world—is what is called prayer. Prayer is needful not as an instrument of deliverance from worldly ills, nor as a means of securing worldly blessings, but as a means of strengthening us in good thoughts. True prayer is important and needful for the soul because in such prayer, in close touch with the Spirit, our thoughts are strengthened. We should pray at all times. Prayer is not meant to appease a god, nor as a means of obtaining material blessings, but as a means of strengthening us in good thoughts. Positive thoughts and prayer help us move out of depression and see clearly the meaning of our lives. Pray on the hour. Have you been frightened, angered, confused, tempted? Make an effort, remember who you are, and what you ought to do. Herein is prayer. This is difficult at first, but the habit may be formed.

7. Good life is impossible without an effort of thought.

Those who are watchful in meditation never die, but the unwatchful are like dead—thus goes a saying of the Buddha. Our true strength is not in impulse, but in the uninterrupted, steady striving after good, which we determine in our thoughts, express in our words, and realize in our actions. The effort of thought is so important because it not only corrects our own life, but is also helpful in the life of others.

Confucius says: "In order to reach the highest good within ourselves, the heart must be corrected. In order to have your heart corrected you must have clear and truthful thoughts."

8. Humans are different from animals only in their capacity to think.

Compared with the world surrounding us, the human being is but a feeble reed, yet, a reed endowed with the capacity to think or reason. That capacity is our most valuable possession, so we should guard it and cultivate it with all our strength. We are different from animals only in our capacity to think. If we apply thought to all that happens to us, nothing in the world can keep us from doing God's will, and we will never complain about our fate or about others. We will never judge others or become slaves to them. We have the power to live our lives reasonably, peacefully, and happily.

CHAPTER TWENTY-FIVE

Self-Denial

The only certain happiness in life
is to live for others.
from *Family Happiness*

The happiness of a person's life is in communion (one-ness) with God and other people through love. Faults prevent this oneness. Faults are caused by our seeking happiness in yielding to the desires of the body rather than in our oneness with God and others. Therefore happiness lies in freedom from faults—the effort to give up the desires of the body.

1. The law of life is in giving up the desires of the body.

Freedom from faults and oneness with all come when we realize we are a spirit instead of a body. In order to achieve this oneness we should be free from faults. The more we yield to the desires of the body, and indulge in such faults as excessive luxury, ill will, greed, sexual unrestraint, and free-loading, the more we are deprived of the spirit. If we give up desires of the body, we strengthen our true spiritual life. As Jesus said, whoever lets go of his bodily life and attachment to self will obtain full spiritual life. And he added, "What good will it be to someone to gain the whole world if he loses his soul?" The fact that we can give up the life of the body clearly shows that there is something in us for the sake of which we give up the body. Self-renunciation (self-denial) is not giving up ourselves, but giving up our bodily desires—transferring ourselves from a bodily to a spiritual level; this does not mean giving up life. Happiness is not in satisfying the demands of the body, but in living on the spiritual level. For animals, bodily satisfaction and the continuation of their kind are the main purpose of life. For humans this is only one level of life. For us, the life of the body is not all of life, but merely something necessary for the true life, which is in the ever-increasing oneness with the Spirit.

2. The fact that death is unavoidable necessarily leads humans to the consciousness of spiritual life which is not subject to death.

The longer we live, the more we realize that our life in the body is limited in time and may end at any moment in death. There is no true life in the body, and whatever we may do for our bodies in this life will not be everlasting. The Spirit which dwells within us does not dwell in us alone, but in all, in the whole world. Realizing this, we no longer place importance on our bodily life, but on developing oneness with the Spirit of God, with that which is everlasting. We must live so that death cannot destroy the work of our life. Money, medicine, arms—nothing we use to make our bodies safe will protect them from death. The insecurity of this life is unavoidable, and deceiving ourselves about this fact only endangers our true life in the spirit. We can liberate ourselves only if we do not cling to material possessions. Busying ourselves with an imaginary security (a security which can never be achieved) makes us forget that nothing we do can *ever* make our life secure. Do not be overly concerned about the body's needs. All we need will be provided.

3. The denial (renouncing) of the body (animal "I") reveals God in the souls of humans.

Consciousness of the body hides the Spirit (which is God) within us. The more we recognize that the spirit is our true self, the more it will be revealed in us. We should give up the body in order to seek God's will, not our own. When we do things for others it should be to obey the will of God, not for our own gain. If we expect nothing from others, they will not disappoint us. Our happiness must not be in the power of others, but in oneness with the Spirit. Desire for all material objects should be given up to the point where they no longer have power over us. This should include giving up the desire for wealth, glory, position, honors, family, and not clinging to children, wife, or brother—none of these belong to us. If we live for our own will, we will always be unhappy; if we give it up, we are bound to be happy.

4. Only denial of self makes it possible to love others.

Only when living for others can we live without living for self. To love others as yourself, you must stop loving yourself above all else; you will then love your neighbor as yourself. You must love others in deed and not in word. We say that we love others, when we love them in word only; yet we love ourselves not in word but in deed. We may forget to help others, but we never forget to help ourselves. In order to love others in deed we must learn to forget ourselves when we are helping others. That which we give to others is ours, that which we withhold belongs to others. If you have deprived yourself and given to others, you have done a good to yourself of which no one can rob you. The time may come when people will learn that it is as easy to live for others as they find it easy to die for others in wars whose purpose is unknown to them.

5. He who employs all his strength only in the gratification of his animal desires destroys his true life.

If you think of yourself alone and seek your own gain in everything, you destroy your true life and cannot be happy. If you would truly live for yourself, live for others. Some people imagine that to give up self is to take away freedom. They do not know that, instead, self-denial allows us to gain true freedom, freeing us from our own self and from serving our own corruption. Our uncontrolled desires are our most cruel rulers: if we give them up we will realize freedom. Self-denial and the animal "enjoyment" of life have nothing in common. Serving our desires keeps us from improving the soul. Realizing our calling (purpose in life) without renouncing our animal desires (personality) is being like a person who has keys to inner apartments within a house without having a key to the outer door. The realization of our calling requires self-denial.

6. Deliverance from sins is possible only through self-renunciation.

After a shift of consciousness occurs and we begin to recognize that we are spiritual beings, we are able to give up bodily desires. The change to spiritual consciousness helps us to see privation and suffering differently. Health, comfort, and outwardly favorable conditions are not necessary for happiness. Nothing can change the happiness of increasing love within. There is nothing more important than inner work with God. Quiet time or meditation in union with the Spirit is essential in helping to check our thoughtless pursuit of animal satisfaction. This consists in not seeking happiness from the life in the body. As we learn to give up small things, it becomes easier to give up greater things. Life is an increasing movement from our self-love as infants to love of God and others in adult life. As we realize that our life is in the spirit and not in the body, we refuse to participate in the wrong deeds of bodily life. If you want with all your soul to correct your life, you will see your life improve. There can be no fullness of life without placing the demands of the spirit above the demands of the body.

7. Laying animal desires aside gives true and secure spiritual blessedness.

The true life of humankind begins only when we seek the good of the spirit and not of the body. The more we remove ourselves from the bodily life to the spiritual life, the more free and joyous our lives become. The fully human life begins when a person seeks fulfillment of the soul rather than of the body. We can do this as we recognize ourselves as spiritual beings. To recognize ourselves as spiritual beings, we must give up the bodily life. Faith requires self-denial; self-denial requires consciousness. As a result of oneness with the Spirit, sacrifice becomes a constant, increasing, and absolute joy. The realization that I *can* because I *should* causes me to feel the loftiness of my true calling. The idea of duty is much simpler, more natural, and clearer to all than the impulse to happiness. That idea of duty is more powerful than all impulses coming from selfishness.

CHAPTER TWENTY-SIX

Humility

. . . we should not demand an eye for an eye,
but when struck on one cheek should offer the other;
should forgive an injury and bear it humbly, and never
refuse anyone a service requested of us.

from *Resurrection*

The greatest human blessing in this world is union with others. Proud people set themselves apart from others, but humble people eliminate all inner obstacles that separate them from the blessing of union with others. Therefore humility is necessary for happiness.

1. We cannot be proud of our deeds because all the good that we do is done not by us but by the higher principle (the Spirit) which dwells in us.

You can only be humble if you know that God dwells within you. If you consider yourself master of your own life, you cannot be humble. Those who see their calling in the service of God are bound to be humble. We are humble when we see ourselves as instruments through which God performs his work. The principal concern in the life of everyone should be to become kinder and better, but how can we become better if we already consider ourselves good? My life is a gift from the Higher Power, and my life's purpose is to do the will of the power which gave me life. If you recognize yourself as a servant instead of a master, then doubt, worry and discontent will immediately give way to certainty, peace and joy.

2. All temptations come from pride.

If we strive after perfection, we will always feel far removed from it because perfection is infinite (endless). Those who know themselves best esteem themselves least. How useful to remember that you are, both in time and space, like a small, insignificant insect; and that your strength is only in understanding your insignificance and therefore being humble. We know more evil things about ourselves then we do about our neighbors. Therefore it should be easy for us to be humble. I am kept humble by guilt from my enjoyment of certain privileges provided through the hardships of others. Every person is a mirror where we can see our defects. Simple people are usually humble, while learned people are mostly self-confident. Peace, freedom, joy of life and lack of fear of death are granted to those who know that in this life they are only servants of their master. My calling is to use the instruments (body and mind) given to me to fulfil my appointed task. All tasks are equal, and I can do nothing more than what is prescribed to me.

3. Humility unites us by means of love.

You are a truly good person if you are not upset because you are unknown, or misunderstood. Those who are good remember their faults and forget their goodness, and those who are evil remember their goodness and forget their faults. If you keep in mind your own faults, you will more easily forgive others. Those who are good and wise regard others as better and wiser than they are. More than anything else on earth, humility generates love. So that people may live well, peace must reign among them. But where each person strives to be higher than the next, there can be no peace. The more humble people are, the easier it is to live in peace.

4. Humility unites us with the higher power.

There is nothing stronger than a humble person, because a humble person, renouncing self, yields to God. Beautiful are the words of the prayer: "Come and dwell in us." So that God may dwell in us, we must do only one thing: diminish ourselves in order to give place to God. If your heart is pure and there is no pride in you, if you are humble, constant, and simple, if you look upon every creature as a friend and love everyone as yourself, if you treat every creature with equal tenderness and love, if you would do good and abandon vanity, then in your heart dwells the Lord of life.

5. How to combat pride.

True humility is difficult. Our heart revolts at the thought of scorn and humiliation. We strive to hide all things that could humiliate us before the eyes of others; we strive to hide them before ourselves. But no matter how difficult true humility may be, it *is* possible. Let us strive to rid ourselves of all things that hinder it. The very defects which are so annoying in others seem as nothing in ourselves. Seeing *our* faults in others is a great help in correcting our own. Nothing is so harmful in striving after moral perfection as self-satisfaction. Avoid the thought that you are better than others and that you have virtues which others lack. Whatever your virtues are they are worthless if you regard yourself better than other people. Compare yourself with supreme perfection only, and not with other people, who may be lower than you. Do not fear humiliations, and bear them in humility. When you start to judge the faults of others, keep before you humiliating remembrances of your own faults. Always view yourself as a learner, until the grave: never think that you are too old to learn.

6. Consequences of pride.

Those who lack humility always condemn others. They see the faults of other people, but their own cravings and vices grow more and more. Self-love makes us want to appear great, important, and good. Such a wrong view is the result of both pride and error in vision. There is one dark spot on our sun: that is the shadow cast by the admiration we feel for our own self. There is nothing more repulsive than a man boasting of his wealth, strength, position, learning, mind, enlightenment, or goodness. People crave to be loved and know that pride is repulsive, and yet they cannot be humble. Why? Because humility is the effect of removing your desires from the material into the spiritual.

7. Humility offers us spiritual happiness and strength in fighting temptations.

There is nothing more helpful and refreshing to the spirit than humiliation meekly and joyfully received. The portal of the temple of truth and blessedness is low. Only they will enter the temple who bow down. The feeblest thing on earth overcomes the strongest; the lowly and humble overcome the exalted and proud. But the higher a person considers himself, the weaker he is. There is nothing more gentle and yielding on earth than water, and yet when it encounters a rock in the stream, the water turns out to be stronger in wearing down the rock. Water is thin, light, and yielding, yet it tears down houses and tosses big ships like nutshells. Air is still thinner, softer, and more yielding, yet it tears out big trees by the roots and raises water in mighty waves. That which is gentle, soft, and yielding overcomes that which is harsh, stern, and unyielding. Similarly, we should be gentle, soft, and yielding; we should be humble in order to overcome what is harsh and unyielding.

Those who would lead others should learn from the rivers that rule the valleys. The rivers are always lower than the valleys. Thus, the leader must be lower than the people. In order to be strong, be like water. In a square vessel it is square, in a round vessel it is round. Because it is so submissive it is at once gentle and strong.

CHAPTER TWENTY-SEVEN

Truthfulness

The hero of my tale—whom I love
with all the power of my soul,
whom I have tried to portray in all his beauty,
who has been, is, and will be beautiful—is Truth.

from "Sevastopol in May"

Superstitions are an obstacle to right living. Freedom from superstitions is only in truthfulness—not only toward others but also toward self.

1. What must be our attitude to established convictions and customs?

Ancient, widely held beliefs accepted on faith must be examined in the light of reason. As we progress and become spiritually more aware, we must examine beliefs which so far have been considered beneficial. To live a true life, one must give up pleasing the world and refuse to be guided by what is accepted as good, but instead carefully search what is the true good. If something is true it can be accepted by everyone (rich or poor, men, women, or children), and should be open to everyone. Truth should be shared with all. Falsehood can never do anyone any good. Every person must reject superstitions (distortions of thought) and examine all beliefs in the light of reason and of the wisdom of humankind.

2. Falsehood, its causes and effects.

It is necessary to be truthful in all matters regardless of their importance or of the consequences they may have. We can change our lives to be in harmony with truth, but we cannot change truth to justify our lives. Falsehood is used to justify a life that is not in agreement with truth. We become free from falsehood only by turning from it and using our reason to seek the truth. Truth is recognized by its simplicity and clearness; falsehood is complex, imaginary, and wordy. No matter whether a person is a famous leader or a very ordinary individual, our every thought, feeling, and spoken word achieves some effect and finds its echo within the human family. Each expression of personal conviction is helpful to someone.

3. On what rests superstition?

Many ancient truths seem to be above doubt because we have never given them serious thought. The more something is considered above doubt and criticism, the more we need to examine its truth. The greatest fault is to abuse reason through using it to conceal or corrupt the truth. The highest falsehood is the establishment of a law which is not subject to investigation and must be believed in blindly. The basis of government authority is force or violence, while the basis of Christianity is love and persuasion. Jesus did not found any church, did not issue any laws, did not set up any external authority, but instead sought to instill the law of God within the hearts of people in order to make them think for themselves. The most absurd and irrational things have been accepted as truths simply because they have been accepted as blind beliefs. Religion cannot validly be excluded from critical examination because of its holiness, or law, because of its authority. Reason may destroy traditions, but it replaces errors with truths.

4. Religious superstitions.

Not knowing God is bad, but it is worse if people worship as God that which is not God. The task of correcting the evil in life includes a necessary first step—each of us should expose religious falsehood and establish religious truth within ourselves. Why do you gather stones and build great temples, seek sacred rivers and forests? Purify yourself, transform yourself into a temple, get rid of negative thoughts, and you will experience the Spirit within you. When we recognize the spirit within us, we recognize ourselves.

Jesus warned us against professional interpreters of scripture (theologians), and urged us not to view scripture experts as "masters." Do not allow anyone to come between your spirit and God. No one can be closer to God than you are. If we do not have personal experience, scripture alone will not banish our fears. Whatever your faith and your prayers, while there is no truth in you, you will not find the path of blessedness. When we recognize the truth within us, we experience a new life. There is much that is good in the Jewish Bible, the *Upanishads,* in the *Gospels,* in the sayings of the Buddha and Confucius, in the writings of the Stoics, but there is more that is useful, accessible, and important to us in the sayings of religious thinkers close to us in time.

5. Reason as an essential human function.

True human worth is in that spiritual principle which is sometimes called reason and sometimes conscience. Reason rises above circumstances of time and place, and contains positive truth. In the midst of what is imperfect, reason sees perfection. It is that which tells each one of us that all people are as precious as we are and their rights are as sacred as ours. It is contrary to all that is prejudiced and selfish in human nature. Reason commands us to receive the truth no matter how much it differs from custom, and no matter how distasteful it is to our pride. It tells us to be just, no matter how unprofitable it may be to us. Reason saves us from slavery to the body. It distinguishes between truth and falsehood, and urges us to live by truth and thus be free. Reason tells us to rejoice in love, in all that is beautiful, holy, and blessed, no matter in whom we find these qualities. It is the highest expression of our thinking nature.

6. Reason—the censor of religious teachings.

Reason was not given to us to solve questions such as why the world exists or why we are alive. It only solves the question of how we are to live. The answer is very clear: so as to do good to ourselves and to others. This is needful to all, and the possibility of living in this way is given to all through the exercise of reason. Reason monitors and rejects all imaginary truths which contradict our reason. In order to know the true religion, it is important not to crush reason— as false teachers would like us to do—but to purify and use it to examine everything. The spirit within you will show you what is false, what is true, and all that you need to know.

CONCLUSION

CHAPTER TWENTY-EIGHT

Misfortunes and Evils

In order to do the will of the Power
which sent us into life, we need restraint,
hard work, struggling, privations, sufferings,
and painful comedowns. . . .
Sorrows and setbacks are great teachers.
from *The Wisdom of Humankind*

All that disturbs the happiness of our bodily life we call evil—ills or misfortunes. Yet all of our life is a gradual process of freeing our soul from that which makes up the body's well-being (happiness). Thus, for one who understands life as it really is, there is no evil.

1. What we call sufferings is a necessary condition of life.

Sufferings that come from misfortunes are a blessing to humans: they make us turn our gaze inward and shake our faith in worldly pleasures. Similarly it is a blessing when, despite pure motives, we fall into disfavor with those around us. It serves as a cure for empty praise. The main reason it is a blessing is that confronting contempt and being deprived of others' love enables us to converse with the Spirit within us.

St. Francis of Assisi teaches that we can find perfect happiness only if we counter hardship and insult with love directed at the person who causes the hardship or inflicts the insult. That happiness is perfect, because it cannot be destroyed, whereas any other form of happiness can be destroyed because we do not have control over it. We would most likely be sorely tempted to accept if a god offered to remove all grief and its causes from our lives. When we are burdened by work or stricken by pain or worry, nothing seems more attractive than a peaceful, calm, and abundant life without toil. But we would soon beg the god to return our suffering to us. Life would be dull and even unbearable if all sorrows, troubles, and failures would disappear, and with them all eagerness and excitement of risk, effort, strain of struggle, and triumph of victory. All that would remain would be to carry out a plan unhindered and achieve success without obstacle. That would soon become just as boring as a game in which we knew in advance that we would win every time.

2. Sufferings stimulate our spiritual life.

We are the Spirit of God clothed in a body. At first we don't realize this and think our life is in the body only, but the longer we live the more we realize that our true life is in the spirit instead of the body. We learn this most easily through sufferings of the body, so sufferings make our life what it could be—a spiritual life. All misfortune leads, though indirectly, to the same goal: the increased realization of the spiritual life in each of us and in humankind at large. We must do the will of the Power which sent us into life—that is, maintain and foster that spark of the Spirit which was entrusted to us. To attain this aim, we need restraint, hard work, struggling, privations, sufferings, and painful comedowns. The only explanation for the strange contradictions of life (disease, senseless dreadful accidents, and other calamities) is that in the depth of their hearts people know that their life is not in the body but in the spirit, and that their sufferings are always needful for the fulfillment of their spiritual life.

3. Sufferings teach humans to maintain a rational attitude to life.

Experiencing sorrows stimulates our spirit and helps it grow. When we meet our lot with strength of the spirit we discover added moral beauty in obstacles, and derive strength from these obstacles. Sorrows are a trial or test to prove how firmly we hold on to our principles. Only after an experience of suffering do we discover our close kinship with other human souls. When we have experienced suffering, we are able to understand the suffering of others. But more than that, our minds clear: we are shown circumstances and achievements of people that were until now hidden to us, and we see clearly what is needful to each. We are enlightened by the sorrows and suffering which we try to avoid. In sorrows we find grains of wisdom that cannot be found in any book. Sorrows and setbacks are great teachers. Not only is everything that happens to us helpful, but it is helpful at the very time when it happens. Until we realize that sufferings are a benefit to us, we have not begun to live the life of reason—the true life. What we regard as misfortunes is mostly good which we have not yet understood.

4. Sicknesses are not a hindrance but a help to true life.

Ills—griefs, sickness, suffering—are the means of gradually transforming the animal within us into a spiritual being. People who are successful, in good health, rich, and who know no injuries or humiliations, frequently have very weak characters; this shows how necessary trials are to us. When we feel weakest in body we are strongest in spirit. No sickness can prevent us from fulfilling our duty. If we cannot serve others by work, we can serve by the example of bearing our suffering with love. If illness attacks, think more about how to live best in the circumstances in which you find yourself and think less about how to cure yourself. A sick person close to death should be informed that death may come soon. Being so informed may stimulate the person toward greater awareness of the spiritual. One who knows life for what it truly is cannot speak of a decrease of life through sickness or old age, cannot grieve over it, any more than one who approaches the light can grieve over the lessening of his shadow in proportion to his approach to the light.

5. So-called ills are only our own errors.

Sufferings come only from our mistakes in thinking, and not from outside causes such as fate or other people. Ills exist only within us, that is, in the place from which they can be removed. Often, when we look at the misfortunes which oppress people in this world, we lose hope in the possibility of improvement in life, and blame God for what has happened. This is a great error. It is important to accept whatever happens to us so we do not lose courage amid life's misfortunes. But it is more important that we do not blame God or fate, and lose sight of the fact that misfortunes are usually caused by our own faults (or by mistakes of others.) Difficulties merely present the opportunities to exercise our goodness, firmness, spiritual strength, patience, courage, and faith. People may escape the misfortunes which are the visitations of God (natural disasters), but there is no escape from those misfortunes which they cause through their own faults.

6. Recognizing that sufferings are beneficial reduces their oppressiveness.

The spiritual life alone gives true happiness. When one accepts the benefits of suffering, its bitterness will vanish. The very misfortunes that trouble us and seem to be a hindrance to our carrying out the task of our life are in themselves the task of our life. If we feel sorry for ourselves, we will be wretched; but if we realize that our task is to live the best life possible in spite of misfortunes, we will immediately gather courage and confidence in place of despondence and despair. (When we accept the task of living life well, sorrows cease to be burdens or obstacles.) It is more important how we receive our fate than what that fate is. No sorrow is as great as the fear of it. Resising sorrows creates suffering. The evil of having an enemy can turn to a blessing by providing an opportunity in learning to love enemies. Time will eventually reveal the healing power which lies in seemingly hopeless losses. Only by recognizing the benefits to be derived from suffering and wholeheartedly accepting suffering can we grow spiritually, which is the whole business of life. In times of sorrow we must both recognize our dependence on the higher will that sent us into the world and seize the opportunity to show our willingness to obey that higher will. Just as Jesus foresaw and accepted as unavoidable the persecution he suffered in his labors, so must those who seek to continue his work accept the persecution they will receive in their attempts to build brotherhood, justice, and truth upon earth. Only by being persecuted will they know they have pursued the right course.

7. Suffering cannot hinder the fulfillment of the will of God.

A person is never closer to God than when experiencing misfortune. Suffering is a blessing to those who believe the ancient proverb that God sends suffering to those he loves. A thinking person ought not to feel grieved about aging and the decrease of physical powers, since physical well-being is unnecessary for the service of God, which is the whole purpose of life. Those who serve God, believing that all that happens is through his will, no longer know any difference between worldly fortune and misfortune. The moment we change the meaning of our life from striving after external blessings to the service of God, we no longer know the difference between misfortune and that which in worldly life is called good fortune. If we say that all things that happen are the will of God, and have faith that the will of God is always good, we will fear nothing and our life will be forever a blessing.

CHAPTER TWENTY-NINE

Death

Love is God, and to die means that I,
a particle of love, shall return to
the general and eternal source.
from *War and Peace*

. . . death is constantly threatening each of us . . .
from "Work, Death, and Sickness"

If we view life as being in the body, our life ends with the death of the body. But if we view life as being in the spirit, we cannot even imagine an end to our life.

1. The life of a person does not cease with bodily death.

Our awakening in the morning is a kind of birth, the course of the day from morning to night a small picture of life, and sleep is something like death. Those who do not understand life imagine that with death all is lost, they fear death and hide from it just as children hide from thunder, although thunder cannot kill them. Faith in immortality (life after death) cannot be gotten from anyone, nor can you force yourself to believe. Death is a change of the envelope to which our spirit is joined. Do not confuse the envelope with its contents. Remember that your life in the body is like a train which is taking you to death. While your body is living through its assigned lifespan and moving toward death, only the spirit within you truly lives.

2. True life is outside time and therefore true life is not in the future.

Time conceals death. Those who live in time cannot imagine time ending. In a way, because we are by our very nature active creatures always involved in pursuits, there should be no room for us to even think of death. We are conscious of something within us which is not subject to time, that is, our life in the present.

3. Death cannot frighten a person who lives the life of the spirit.

Suffering and death appear as misfortunes to us only when we accept the law of the body as the law of our life. If we lived a fully spiritual life, there would be neither suffering nor death for us. The body is like walls which confine the spirit and limit its freedom. The spirit continually tries to break these walls, and the whole life of a rational person is in pushing these walls apart, in releasing the spirit from the captivity of the body. If all my life is filled with worldly desires and their gratification, then I will fear what puts a stop to the pleasure derived from the gratification of those desires. But if these desires are transformed within me and replaced with my desire to do God's will, then for me there is only life and there is no death. Death is the spirit's final complete release. Therefore death is not terrible, but a joy to one who lives the true life. The more we live in the spirit the better our life is, and the less we fear death. To a saint there is no death.

4. Humans must live by that which is immortal in them.

When we live the life of the body, we live like a hired servant in a house, but when we live in the spirit, we live like a child of the owner of the house. If we realize that in addition to having a mortal body which will die, we have an immortal soul which is everlasting, we will pay more attention to what is immortal (the spirit) than to what is mortal (the body). Our bodies grow feeble and old, and die, but our spirits are gaining spiritual vigor, growth, and birth. Love eliminates not only the dread of death, but even the thought of it. If there is a God and life everlasting ahead of us, all things are changed. We see good in evil, light in darkness, and hope in despair. True life begins when we live without thinking of what awaits us, but only to show the love within us. Do the works of love and there will be no death for you.

5. Being mindful of death enhances spiritual life.

Falsely-directed medical skill is that which aims at postponing death at all costs and in all cases, making people hope they can escape death, and thus depriving them of an important stimulus to moral life. One who lives after being cured of a mortal illness is like a truck which has been pulled from a mudhole and left on the wrong side of it. It cannot escape the mudhole, since it must go past it again. In order to encourage yourself to do good, remember that you must soon die. Then you surely will not deceive, lie, criticize, judge, steal, or feel hatred toward others. If you are mindful of death, you do only the simplest of good deeds—help, comfort, and show love to others. Such acts are those that are needed most and give most joy. To be ready for death means to live right. The consciousness of approaching death teaches us to bring our affairs to completion. Practicing love in the present is the only important task. Set the object of your life not in the concerns of the body, but in the spirit; not in more learning, wealth, and glory, but in more goodness, love, and freedom from the body. Then old age and death will no longer be fearful.

6. Dying.

We have no control over death, but the process of dying is in our power. Our dying may be good or bad. We must strive to die right. This is needful for those who survive. The most precious activities of life, most needful to ourselves and others, are carried on in the closing years of old age. Try to live right and when old, try to die right—to die willingly. All things in life seem simple; all things are interconnected, are of one order, and explain one another. But death appears to be something exceptional, a break in the chain of that which is simple, clear, and intelligible in life. Most people try not to think about death. This is a big mistake. Life must be so harmonized with death that life has something of the solemnity and mystery of death, and death has something of the clearness, simplicity, and obviousness of life.

CHAPTER THIRTY

After Death

*"What death?" There was no fear because there was
no death. In place of death there was light.
"Death is finished," he said to himself. "It is no more!"*
from *The Death of Ivan Ilych*

What will be after death? We know the body will decay and turn to dust. But what will become of the spirit? "What will become" relates to time, but the spirit is not in time. Spirit *was* not, nor *will be*. It only *is*. Without it nothing would be.

1. Carnal death is not the end of life, but simply a transformation.

Death can be one of the following:

a) disappearance of consciousness, like a deep sleep without dreams;

b) transfer of the spirit from one being to another;

c) ceasing to be separate beings and merging with God.

Death is the final change of our body—and there is no reason to fear it any more than we feared earlier bodily changes. We know that our life is not in the changes of the body, but in that which dwells in our body, in our spirit. The spirit can have no beginning or end, because it alone *is*. If our life is striving after spiritual perfection, we cannot think of death as the interruption of that striving. That which is on the way to perfection cannot be destroyed; it can only be changed. Various thinkers have come to the conclusion that we have possibilities that go far beyond earthly life, and that there is no death. To think that we die because our body is dying is to think the workman is dead because his tools have worn out.

2. The nature of the change in existence which occurs with the death of the body is unfathomable to the human mind.

We often try to see death as a passage into something, and try to picture what exists after death. We do not know what will become of the soul after death of the body. One thing is certain: just as we came from somewhere when we entered into life, we shall return to that same source in death; thus death is a blessing. As a person's life is a series of changes, so birth and death are changes which sometimes we do not understand. If we believe that all that has happened to us in our life has happened for our blessing, we cannot fail to believe that what happens to us when we die will also be for our blessing. When we say "Thy will be done" and know God's will is love, we need give no thought to what will be after death.

3. Death—a release.

Death is the end of the body which contained the spirit. As death destroys the coffin-like body, the spirit is freed to live. We know that death is a natural process in which the physical body is abandoned by that which animated it; but we cannot know whether that animation passes into a new form of life or unites with the creative energy which first gave it life.

If we live in a constant attempt to overcome the cravings of the body for the sake of the strength and purity of the spirit, then death is the final release of the spirit, which continues, from the body, which fails. There is no reason to fear death—to do so is illogical. If death is a total end, then life is always so short that it is not of great importance anyway; whereas if the spirit does continue, then death is merely a change, a discarding of an old tool, a freeing of one's essential being (spirit)—in short, a release.

4. Birth and death are the boundaries beyond which our life is unknown to us.

Birth and death are the same in many ways. Both, though not the ends of life, are boundaries beyond which we have no knowledge of our life. The process by which an infant leaves the womb and enters into the life we know holds many similarities to the process in which a dying person leaves this life for something else. Someone undergoing the process of birth, life and death is like a person who leaves home (God) for the day, during which he or she works, plays, and learns, and then returns home (to God) for the night. We fear this major change called death; yet just such a change, called birth, had results so good that now we hate to part from our present state.

5. Death frees the spirit from the confines of personality.

Throughout our lives, we attempt to expand the boundaries of our consciousness to include others. Death completes this process by freeing us from the one-sidedness of our personality (which has kept us from fully reaching out and including others). Personality is the shape our bodies inflict upon our spirits, and that which causes one to see oneself as separate from others—a dream from which we hope to awake in death. Death is joyful to those tired of being separate from the world. All people create their own awareness of the outside world; therefore, no two people are separated from the world in the same way. In death, at least the way in which one sees the world will change. It follows, then, that at the very worst the way in which we feel separated from the world changes—if, in fact, we continue to feel separated from the world at all.

6. Death reveals that which had been unfathomable.

The longer we live, the more life reveals itself to us, and the more information becomes known to us. But in death, all is revealed that we can know. The achieving of this insight explains the expression of simple peace often found on the face of a dying person. The dying person is already attuned to the eternal, and the person's nature consequently reveals itself. Death reveals the individual's true self completely.

CHAPTER THIRTY-ONE

Life Is a Blessing

"To live! I want to live," he said to himself.
from *The Death of Ivan Ilych*

Our life and its blessedness (happiness) consist in the ever closer union of our spirit with God and others from whom it has been separated through the body. This union is reached by the spirit as it reveals itself through love, and frees itself more and more from the body. As we realize this, life becomes constant blessedness in spite of all misfortunes, sufferings, and ailments.

1. Life is the highest blessing attainable.

We often disregard the blessings of this life, expecting something better somewhere else. But no such higher blessing can exist anywhere, for the blessing of life that we have been given is the greatest possible blessing. To make every moment of life the best possible, no matter whether it is favorable or unfavorable, is the art of living. Since God desires our blessedness, in striving for our blessedness we do that which God desires of us, and therefore fulfill his will.

2. True happiness is in the present life and not in the life beyond the tomb.

Do not believe that this life is but a transition into another world, and our happiness lies only in that other world. This is untrue. We should be happy in this world right here. In order to be happy in this world, we must only live as God desires. You must not say that in order for you to live well, everyone else must live according to God's will. This is wrong; if *you* live according to God's will and make every effort of your own, you will be happy, and others will also be better off. If we beg things of God, we have not done what we were to do: fulfill God's law and be thankful for the life and happiness we have been given.

3. True happiness you can find only within yourself.

A wise man remarked: "I have covered the earth in my travels seeking happiness. I searched for it day and night without ceasing. Once when I had despaired of finding it, an inner voice told me: happiness is in thyself. I obeyed the voice and found true and unchangeable happiness." Happy are those who call nothing their own but their spirit. Happy are they even if they live among covetous, evil, and hateful people, for none can take their happiness away from them. The wise person seeks everything within self, the madman everything from others.

4. The true life is the spiritual life.

Fulfillment (well-being) of our spiritual "I" depends on our submission to God's will. Misfortunes or ills come from considering only our material personality as truly existing. Those who define the aim of their lives as releasing their spiritual selves from bodily limitations cannot be dissatisfied. Ever-increasing consciousness of God in my self is what gives significance to my life. Achieving increasing consciousness of God within self is a reasonable spiritual task—as opposed to other tasks which mean an excessive burden for us to carry.

Human life is a constant reunion of the soul with God. Whether we understand or not, whether we will it or not, this reunion is being unceasingly accomplished through the condition which we call human life. Those who do not understand their calling and do not wish to fulfill it are like stubborn animals which the master must drag by a rope attached to the neck into the refuge that has food and shelter. Though they struggle and choke themselves, they will be taken to the place to which all must come. Those who do understand their calling and wish to fulfill it are like animals which go willingly and gladly where the master leads, knowing that nothing but good can result from obeying. Craving anything besides the perfecting of myself will remain an unsatisfied desire. To be blessed, to have eternal life, to abide in God, to be saved—all refer to the same thing: it is the solution of the problem of life.

5. Wherein is true happiness?

There are few true blessings. Only that is a true blessing and good which is a blessing and good for all. Therefore it is needful to desire only that which is in accord with the common good. To do good is one occupation which will surely benefit us. Those who direct their activities toward such an aim will be blessed. This blessing is an immediate inner reward, the betterment of the soul, and not something outside us or in the future. The only help we can get is the help coming from our leading a good life.

6. Blessedness lies in Love.

Longing for happiness teaches us the purpose of our lives, and what to do in life. In order to be truly happy, only one thing is needed: love—to love all, the good and the bad. Love others continually. Make the object of your life to increase love, and you will find that it will always be in your power to achieve happiness. My life is not my own, and therefore my own happiness cannot be my life's aim; its only aim can be fulfilling the wish of the spirit that sent me into life. That wish is for me to practice love toward all. There is joy in loving even disagreeable people. Duty in the present and death in the future may seem depressing and dreadful, yet if you strive for ever greater loving communion with others and with God, that which had seemed dreadful becomes the greatest happiness.

7. The more we live for body alone, the more surely we miss true blessedness.

People seek happiness in power, in knowledge, in pleasure, but true happiness is not in any particular things which may be possessed by some few only. True happiness must be such that all may possess it at the same time without lack or envy, and none may lose it against their will. Love provides a basis for happiness. Do not seek true happiness in distant lands, in riches, or in honors. Do not beg or cringe before others or struggle against them in order to attain happiness. True happiness cannot be bought or asked for, but is given freely. We should be grateful that the things that are needful to us are easy and the things that are needless are difficult. That which we need most of all is happiness, and to be happy is the easiest thing of all. It is only that which is in our power, and no one can rob us of our happiness.

8. The one who is unconscious of the blessedness of life has failed to fulfill the law of life.

If the life of the people is not full of joy, it is because they fail to do that which is needful in order to make life a constant joy. If people say that though doing good they feel unhappy, it merely proves that what they consider good is not good. If we are unhappy it is our own fault. People are only unhappy when they desire something they cannot have: but they are happy when they desire something they can have. We desire some things that are not always in our power to have (such as things that do not belong to us, and things which others can take away from us). Only those things are in our power with which neither anyone nor anything can interfere. True happiness comes from our efforts to come closer to spiritual perfection, and these efforts are always in our power.

We have no right to be dissatisfied with this life. If it seems to us that we are dissatisfied with it, it merely proves that we have good grounds to be dissatisfied with ourselves. People who stray from the one true path of life are dissatisfied with life and frequently destroy themselves, because, having strayed from the right path, they refuse to acknowledge their mistake.

9. Only the fulfillment of the law of life yields blessing.

We must make it our first rule to be happy, contented, and joyful. We should be ashamed of our discontent as though of an evil action, and know that if something is wrong with us, we should not tell others or complain, but rather correct that which is wrong. Fulfilling the law of God, the law of love which yields supreme blessing, is possible in every condition of life. No matter how troubled we may be, however overcome with griefs and misfortunes, we only need realize and receive in our hearts the teaching that life and its blessings consist in the union of the soul with that from which it is separated by the body: with the souls of others and with God, and all apparent ills will vanish at once. Life will immediately change from agony to blessedness.

Tolstoy's Search for Wisdom

Famous to the general public as a novelist, Leo Tolstoy was also a foremost sage of the late 19th and early 20th centuries. His achievements in this latter capacity are less known to a broader circle of readers. Furthermore, a naive but rather widespread misperception has divided the great writer's works into two supposedly watertight parts—the pre-1880 period (comprising mostly fiction), and the post-1880 period (comprising mostly nonfictional writings). Most readers have overlooked the continuity between these two parts because of a misinterpretation of the deep spiritual crisis which Tolstoy underwent in 1879-1880. This misinterpretation claims that radically new elements were then introduced into Tolstoy's values and that an entirely new philosophical and supposedly austere dimension suddenly appeared in his works.

On the other hand, at least one perceptive critic has correctly stressed that "from the first, Tolstoy's life was an ethical quest . . ." and his imaginative writing was the reflection of that quest. Tolstoy's quest is reflected in several of his fictional works: in the search for authentic happiness in *Family Happiness* (1859), in the Rousseauistic pursuit of the natural and pure life in *The Cossacks* (1863), in the continuing search for values and commitment on the part of Prince Andrei and Pierre Bezukhov in *War and Peace* (1869), and in Levin's anguished questions and doubts in *Anna Karenina*.

The continuity between the earlier work and the post-1880 themes was not overlooked by the prominent nineteenth-century English critic Matthew Arnold who, considering the concerns present in Tolstoy's *A Confession* and other nonfictional writings of the 1880s, remarked: "All this is but development, sometimes rather surprising, but always powerful and interesting, of what we have already had in the pages of *Anna Karenina.* What is new in the recent books is the solution and cure announced."

Far from being unrelated therefore, Tolstoy's religious-philosophical system and his supreme achievement as a writer of fiction are intimately interconnected, finding their integration in what the British critic E. B. Greenwood has called "Tolstoy's comprehensive vision." A close study of a significantly broad spectrum of texts from Tolstoy's fiction *and* nonfiction reveals the essential unity of his spiritual vision as it spanned several decades. It is generally acknowledged that a striving for moral integrity and great sharpness of vision are present in all of Tolstoy's fictional works since the semi-autobiographical trilogy, *Childhood, Boyhood,* and *Youth* (1852-1857). Although analyzed by literary critics mainly as an aesthetic category, Tolstoy's lucid vision had the power to inspire the program of committed and ardent social action that was the necessary outcome of his religious-philosophical views.

What did occur in the 1880s is that, as a result of the enormous international reputation acquired both through his fiction and some of his more recent writings, Tolstoy began to command considerable respect and admiration. Readers on all continents sent him thousands of letters every year. Indeed, Tolstoy found himself promoted to the role of a teacher of life. For most of us, as Ernest J. Simmons has stated, it is difficult today "to believe that Tolstoy was at one time regarded as the conscience of humanity, the greatest single moral force in the world during the last years of the nineteenth century." A thinker of such considerable stature has been for the most part ignored over a period of many years, during which both the Soviet Union and the West (though for different reasons) have neglected his philosophy and focused almost exclusively on his achievements as a writer of fiction. The current re-evaluation of Tolstoy and his work is reflected in the statement by Richard Gustafson: "We have not taken Tolstoy seriously. We have read him and written about him, but have not come to grips with him . . . we do not in the main see Tolstoy whole: the writer and the thinker."

Tolstoy's nonfictional works comprise seven book-length studies, as well as scores of essays, articles, pamphlets, statements, and addresses. Tolstoy's religious philosophy is a highly thoughtful and original formulation of the common denominator of the major spiritual doctrines and moral philosophies of humankind. Tolstoy was fully familiar with all the major spokesmen of what Aldous Huxley later called the "Perennial Philosophy" (translated from German philosopher Leibniz's *philosophia perennis),* or the Highest Common Factor of all of the world's theologies and moral philosophies.

In formulating the essence of religion, Tolstoy drew upon seven major religious-philosophical systems. Beginning in the 1880s, Tolstoy undertook a most thorough study of Christianity, Judaism, Islam, Buddhism, Taoism, and the Baha'i faith (which during Tolstoy's lifetime started establishing its credentials as a major religion).

In *A Confession,* Tolstoy described his early participation as a youth in the life of the traditional Russian Orthodox Church. He traced his growing disillusionment with its set practices and ceremonies, his eventual loss of faith, and his subsequent agnosticism. Many years later, in his late forties, Tolstoy experienced a spiritual crisis that led him back to the Russian Orthodox Church. With great eagerness he examined its spiritual wisdom, diligently attended services, and kept Church observances such as fasts and confession. Within Orthodoxy Tolstoy discovered the staunch faith of the Russian peasants—a faith whose pristine or primeval spirit Tolstoy felt was a source of authenticity. Nevertheless, he was disappointed by the inconsistent and unsatisfactory replies given to vital existential issues either by the Russian Orthodox catechism or by the priests and monks whom he consulted. Gradually he freed himself from the official Orthodox Church to retain what he felt to be the true essence of Christ's teachings.

At least until the 1890s Tolstoy viewed Christianity as a privileged formulation of the Perennial Philosophy. He explained to a correspondent that Christianity went beyond the other world religions in "preaching the possibility and necessity of founding the Kingdom of God on earth." However, in the 1900s, Tolstoy tended in many instances to speak of "religion" rather than "Christianity" in order to avoid restrictive references to Christianity as a would-be unique form of religious experience. It should be noted that during the latter part of his life he believed in a Christianity shorn of the supernatural, of conceptual dogmatic elaborations, and of ritual. For Tolstoy, such eliminations were essential for religion to be authentic.

In the 1880s Tolstoy also turned his attention to Judaism and its scriptures. Under the guidance of a learned Rabbi of Moscow, he pursued a very careful and systematic study of Hebrew and apparently achieved an adequate enough command to be able to read the Judaic Bible in that language. The

Rabbi pointed out to him the considerable extent to which the moral message of Christianity was already contained, in all essentials, in the Jewish scriptures.

Three short stories written by Tolstoy in 1901 in aid of the victims of the pogroms attest to his interest in Judaism and his concern for the plight of persecuted Jews. One of the stories in particular, "Esarhaddon, King of Assyria," contains an important summation of the notion of the unity of life—a cardinal point in Tolstoy's religious philosophy.

Tolstoy's earliest exposure to the language and culture of Islam came when, in 1842-44, he studied Arabic and Turkish with a view to admission into the University of Kazan. Once enrolled, he continued for a time to study these subjects under eminent teachers of Oriental languages, literatures, and history. Insights gained during these early contacts with Islamic culture were to be reflected in a number of Tolstoy's literary works, such as *The Cossacks, Prisoner of the Caucasus,* and *Hadji Murad.*

Even after Tolstoy abandoned a career as a student of Oriental languages, he was to maintain throughout his life a thoughtful interest in the cultural areas where these languages are spoken. Through his careful reading of the *Qur'an* (*Koran*), he developed great respect for its spiritual message—the call to brotherly love and deference to God's Providence. However, he criticized the practice among Muslims of "belief" in the sense of "blind faith in Mohammed and the *Qur'an.*" He was also critical of orthodox Islam for its intolerance towards those of other faiths. Tolstoy therefore called upon Muslims to ". . . take from the *Qur'an* only that which agrees with reason and the conscience of all men." He used several Arabic proverbs in the anthologies of the world's wisdom, such as *Thoughts of Wise Men for Daily Use,*

A Cycle of Readings, and *The Wisdom of Humankind,* that he composed from the 1880s until his death.

In the 1880s and 1890s Tolstoy read the works of several scholars of Hinduism and became acquainted with portions of Hindu scriptures, in particular the fundamental Hindu classic, the *Bhagavad Gita.* While having the greatest respect for the formulation of the Perennial Philosophy to be found in the Hindu scriptures, he remarked on the degradation that institutionalized Hinduism had undergone. These and similar impressions about Hinduism Tolstoy would share with a number of correspondents from India.

Tolstoy's most important exchange with a practitioner of Hinduism was his correspondence with young Mohandas Karamchand (later, Mahatma) Gandhi. They exchanged several letters, and their dialogue was of significance for Tolstoy and crucial for Gandhi. Tolstoy felt that Gandhi's experiments with nonviolent resistance in South Africa were the most important endeavors being undertaken in the world at the time. Gandhi spoke in very strong terms of the decisive influence that Tolstoy's *The Kingdom of God Is Within You* had upon him, acting as a catalyst that made him a firm believer in nonviolence. Gandhi was to say of Tolstoy: "He was the most truthful man of this age . . . He was the greatest apostle of nonviolence that the present age had produced." Acknowledging his debt to the Russian sage in most forceful terms, Gandhi regarded Tolstoy as his mentor or guide.

Tolstoy's first encounter with Buddhism occurred at an early age when, in 1847, as a young student at the University of Kazan, he was hospitalized. One of his ward mates was a Buddhist who, abiding by his principles of nonviolence, had refrained from fighting back or defending himself when attacked by a robber on the highway. As the episode was narrated to him, Tolstoy was deeply moved.

Tolstoy was well acquainted with at least a certain portion of the Buddhist scriptures, especially with the famous collection of the Buddha's sayings, the *Dhammapada*. This acquaintance was developed in particular in the 1880s, when Tolstoy was working on his project of composing and publishing a series of books on Eastern religions and thinkers.

Tolstoy found numerous elements in Buddhism to be in harmony with his own philosophy (or rather, with the Perennial Philosophy as he perceived it): the prohibition of killing and condemnation of war, violence, and envy; the advocacy of nonresistance to evil by force; of the need to achieve a certain degree of withdrawal from the material, external world; of the need to attain self-knowledge; of compassion and mercy; the call to simplify one's lifestyle; the invitation to scorn riches; and the notion of doing good and radiating compassion as the prime dynamism of life. Tolstoy once remarked to a friend: "The Buddha says that happiness consists in doing the maximum good to others . . . it is really so: happiness is possible only when you give up the striving for personal, selfish desire."

Tolstoy began studying the philosophy of Lao-Tzu (Lao Tse) in the early 1870s. The work traditionally attributed to Lao Tzu (and known to scholars as the *Lao Tzu*) is *The Way of Life*, or the *Tao Te Ching*. Tolstoy's fascination with the essential message regarding the Tao (the Way) is reflected in his essay of 1893, "Non-Acting." This Chinese doctrine found the source of social and political evils in man's upsetting the natural order of the Universe, or Tao, through his ceaseless creation of complex artifacts and institutions of so-called "civilization." The resulting imbalance can be corrected through thoughtful practice of *wu wei*, or non-acting, on the numerous occasions when our indiscriminate and unnecessary action is what generates trouble in the world.

Tolstoy judged the typical nineteenth-century belief in constant activity and work to be related to the cult of progress and science, which functioned as a secular religion. Underlying the unrelenting and mechanical approach to work is routine, which, in spiritual terms is opposed to the force of reason and love that draws humanity toward enlightenment. Echoing the *Tao Te Ching,* Tolstoy appeals to humans to achieve a harmonious balance between activity and passivity by foregoing action in cases when it is harmful. In this context Tolstoy makes an allusion to the parable in the Gospel that portrays the individuals who are unable to pay attention to essential spiritual realities (the Kingdom of God) because they are excessively involved in various worldly pursuits. Through prayer and meditation man is able to "look around him, think of the results of his work, and ask himself: What am I? Why do I live?"

Tolstoy familiarized himself with the Baha'i faith as it was evolved by its major exponent, Mirza Khossein-Ali, otherwise known as Baha'u'llah (1817-1892). Tolstoy discovered that Baha'u'llah, while still advocating a single world government as an ultimate goal for humankind, condemned the movement's earlier struggles against the Persian state. Baha'u'llah also protested the division of humankind into "believers" and "non-believers," and proclaimed the equality of all human beings, friendship and brotherhood among nations, and the prohibition of warfare. These elements in the doctrine had strong appeal for Tolstoy, as well as Baha'u'llah's fostering of a single world religion based on universal love for one's neighbor. In general Tolstoy believed that the Baha'i faith had a "great future." It had rejected the "old Muslim superstitions" and had not replaced them with new ones, and it continues to uphold "its principal ideas of brotherhood, equality, and love."

As Aldous Huxley was to do after him, Tolstoy found confirmation of the tenets of the major religions in the writings of moral philosophies. He found such confirmation in the works of two of the greatest thinkers of antiquity: Epictetus (the author of the *Manual* or *Enchiridion*) and Marcus Aurelius (the author of *Meditations*). Among modern philosophers, Rousseau and Kant especially influenced Tolstoy's thought.

In the early 1850s, Tolstoy nurtured, as did Rousseau before him, the dream of founding a new religion (a Christianity purged of dogma and mysticism) and of spreading happiness on earth. Tolstoy was inspired by Rousseau's conviction, as expressed in *The Creed of a Savoyard Priest*, that our spiritual and religious needs are legitimate and not merely the result of superimposed superfluities.

Kant, author of *Religion within the Limits of Reason Alone* (1793), also had a decisive impact on the Russian writer. In a recent study, Gary Jahn has demonstrated that Tolstoy, in the Kantian tradition, reflected on theory of knowledge, metaphysics, and ethics, as well as the problems of the modern age. Tolstoy was clearly in sympathy with the ethics taught by Kant, and, like Kant, distinguished between practical reason and pure reason. Especially in his later works, Tolstoy was at some pains to comment upon the difficulty we humans have in perceiving with due gravity the absolute inevitability of our own death. In this connection, Tolstoy quoted Kant with approval "to the effect that man is unmoved by the thought of death because he is by nature an active being and consequently death, the absolute cessation of activity is an inappropriate and perhaps incomprehensible subject of his meditations." Most importantly, Tolstoy adopted the Kantian notion that there exists one true rational religion "in which all particular religious creeds participate to a greater or

lesser extent and which consists solely of moral precepts."
Tolstoy found in Kant a confirmation of his own insistence
upon morality as the essence of religion.

Rather like the unified synthesis of religious and philosophical doctrines that Aldous Huxley was to present in his
volume *The Perennial Philosophy*, Tolstoy's vision encompassed
the essential continuity between the major religions and the
moral philosophers, between, for example, the Christian
catechism of self-improvement and Marcus Aurelius' teachings on self-improvement. At the same time, Tolstoy's formulation of the essence of religion is not just the effect of
an intellectual experience, but is also the result of his existential quest, as revealed in *A Confession*.

Tolstoy had come to understand the fundamental truth
that life is one. In the short story "Esarhaddon, King of
Assyria" (1903), he reveals this truth. Esarhaddon dreams
that he is in turn physically the same as his enemy, Lailie, and
as a colt slain during a hunt. An old man explains to Esarhaddon:

> You thought life dwelt in you alone but . . . you have
> seen that by doing evil to others you have done it to
> yourself also. Life is one in them all, and yours is but a
> portion of this same common life. . . . You can only
> improve life in yourself by destroying the barriers that
> divide your life from that of others, and by considering
> others as yourself and loving them.

In an earlier book-length statement entitled *On Life*, Tolstoy writes that true life is beyond spatial and temporal
determinations and limitations; it is not limited to life in the
flesh. A person's life is not extinguished at the time of that
person's physical death; the memory left by any person
endures to the extent that his or her life achieved conformity
with reason, and was manifested as and through love.

For Tolstoy, true religion consists in what is common to the various major faiths—the fundamental message insisting on the need to forget or transcend the small self, or what he calls "animal personality" (*zhivotnaia lichnost'*), through the practice of brotherly love. In *My Religion* Tolstoy affirms the reality of an inner God revealing His presence to humans through the voice of conscience. The ultimate purpose of our lives is not to cater to our lower animal nature, but to serve "the power which our higher nature recognizes." Tolstoy supports the precept that is at the center of both Judaic and Christian morality: "Love God with all your heart, with all your soul, and with all your mind, and love your neighbor as yourself." He made a plea for a common religion for all of humankind, a highly refined, supra-denominational universal religion; as one critic affirmed decades ago, on this "rests his universal significance." Aware of the inherent unity of religions, Tolstoy stated: "According to my conviction, there is only one true religion. This true religion of humankind has not yet revealed itself fully, but it appears in fragmentary fashion in all creeds."

Tolstoy defines religion as "a relation, in accordance with reason and knowledge, which man establishes with the infinite life surrounding him—and it is such as binds his life to that infinity, and guides his conduct." In another formulation Tolstoy declares: "By 'true religion' I mean a religion that is accessible to all humans, that is grounded in reason (which is common to all humans), and that is therefore binding for all."

Ignorance of true religion is a cause of evil, and only reason can dispel it. Therefore, the moral laws and prescriptions that compose true religion should be founded on reason. In a letter Tolstoy writes: "I can only be convinced by what I know by myself and can verify through argument and inner experience within myself."

The basic principles of true religion, found in all the major religions, are:

a) that in us dwells a spark of spiritual awareness which we, by our way of living, can increase or decrease in ourselves;

b) that to increase this spiritual spark we must suppress our passions and increase love in ourselves; and

c) that the practical means to attain this result is to do to others as you would they do to you.

After years of studying the Gospels and considerable reflection, Tolstoy concluded that the practical demands emanating from the doctrine of Jesus could be presented in five laws or precepts. He regards Christianity as an expression (the one most accessible to Westerners) of the universal religion, and viewed these five points as having a universal rather than a narrow, denominational significance.

The first law is that not only we should not kill (according to the precept from the Judaic Bible) but should not even be angry with any fellow human being; should not consider anyone worthless; and if we have quarrelled with anyone, should make it up with that person before bringing our gift to God, that is, before praying.

The second law is not to commit adultery; and not leave the spouse to whom one is united.

The third law is that we should never bind ourselves by oath and thus compromise our moral freedom. (Tolstoy sees Jesus as appealing to us not to abdicate our reason and our conscience, as one does when taking any oath of total obedience and allegiance, for example to an army commander.)

The fourth law is that we should not demand an eye for an eye, but when struck on one cheek should offer the other; should forgive an injury and bear it humbly; and never refuse anyone a service desired of us. (In numerous texts, Tolstoy denounces the various forms of coercion, compulsion, and violence in modern society.)

The fifth law is that we should neither hate our enemies nor fight them, but love them, help them, and serve them. (Such a practice means that in due time we will have no enemies left, but will have only friends, or brothers and sisters.)

It is clear that for Tolstoy the common denominator among the major religions—the Perennial Philosophy—is that which unites people of different faiths. He therefore rejects those aspects of religion—ritual, belief in the supernatural, and dogma—that separate human beings from one another:

a) *Ritual* risks becoming repetitive and mechanical, thus hindering our spiritual inquiry, discovery, and progress. Like the rites that they perform, ministers and priests, often regarded as privileged individuals and forming a special class of human beings, act as unnecessary intermediaries between humans and God. (One could criticize Tolstoy's de-emphasizing and underestimation of collective forms of religious activity, such as church meetings and worship gatherings, as an overly purified and rarefied approach to religion—an approach obviously too austere for many.)

b) Dwelling on the *miracles* found in the Gospel (as well as those attributed to Krishna, the Buddha, and other founders of religions and saints) is unduly removing oneself from the *live inspiration and focus of true religion:* service to God through serving people.

c) Tolstoy does not accept the authoritarian imposition of a *dogmatic body of knowledge* by a church, for this imposition overrules the supreme authority: individual conscience and reason. For Tolstoy, complex conceptual elaborations belong to the realm of Kant's Pure Reason and cannot replace Kant's Practical Reason or Blaise Pascal's "reason of the heart" as a means of comprehending reality. (Tolstoy did not consider his own formulation of the essential points of the teaching of Jesus as being dogmatic, in that this teaching is based on, and verifiable through, common and universal experience.)

At the age of twenty-seven, Tolstoy had made an entry in his diary about a notion that occurred to him—"a great, a stupendous idea"—to whose realization he felt capable of dedicating his whole life. That idea was "the founding of a new religion corresponding to the [current level of] development of humankind: the religion of Christ, but purged of all dogma and mystery, a practical religion, not promising future bliss but realizing bliss on earth." (Diary entry for March 7, 1855)

Three decades later, Tolstoy was well on his way to elaborating this new religion, and during the last twenty-five years of his life he progressed in articulating and refining it. That new religion—the essence of the wisdom of all ages—was Tolstoy's teaching of universal love and nonviolence as presented in *The Wisdom of Humankind*.

That teaching is a crisp and sharp formulation of the core message of Jesus of Nazareth, although Tolstoy made it clear that we should not be bound by any one historical revelation. He felt we should also stay attuned to the more recent ways in which the Spirit currently makes itself heard.

Universal love and compassion was presented by Tolstoy in a spirit similar to that of Jesus, the Buddha, and other spiritual guides. His strongest claims to originality lie in his evolving and presenting in compelling contemporary terms a teaching of nonviolence based on the message of the Buddha, Jesus, and Lao Tzu in the Taoist Way of Life.

Tolstoy feels that we need guidelines—a map, a chart, or a compass—to show us the way through life. We need "general guidance for our conduct," an "explanation of the meaning of life," "the consciousness of our relation to the

Infinite, and the guidance of conduct derived from such consciousness."

Such guidance is provided by what Tolstoy calls "the Law of Love," the enabling and nurturing principle which is the opposite of what he terms the Law of Aggression or the Law of Violence. For him, the Law of Love is "the supreme law of human life," the "foundation of everything," and "the highest law that guides human life." Our well-being lies in the fulfilment of that Law; "only through fulfilling that Law do we become truly free."

This new religion reminds us that our welfare or well-being lies only in our achieving unity, and that "unity cannot be attained by violence." This universal religion goes against "the obsolete law of revenge," against "the application of crude revenge" as propounded by the Law of Violence. Violence is the result of the "animal instincts which divide," and leads to disunity or division, the opposite of the higher spiritual aim—unity. Violence also is both the source and the outcome of class hatred and national hatreds and other forms of divisiveness.

An increase of Love can only occur if we practice "inner labor upon ourselves" which alone makes us free and powerful, and if we destroy everything which prevents that manifestation of Love, such as mistakes or passions. The task of each one of us is to arrange our life in accord with the supreme religious law, the Law of Love. In order to increase the Love factor, we should begin to live not for external aims, but the fulfillment of the real calling of our lives.

Finally, it should be mentioned that Tolstoy had little patience with any would-be religious tradition or system that does not come to grips with pressing social issues. Perhaps that feeling on the part of Tolstoy is most succintly conveyed by Martin Luther King, Jr. when he said:

Any religion that professes to be concerned with the soul of men and is not concerned with the slums that damn them, the economic conditions that strangle them, and the social conditions that cripple them is a dry-as-dust religion. Such a religion is the kind the Marxists like to see—an opiate of the people.

On the basis of such feelings, in various statements Tolstoy emphasizes service. Tolstoy's conception of religion stresses appropriate action to redress injustice in the world. The fact that it is an existential, action-oriented doctrine is readily seen from its concern with the practical-social applications and consequences of the moral principles. These range from practical decisions to be made in everyday life (such as acts of civil disobedience) to choices pertaining to such diverse fields as education, law, science, and the arts.

One of the most powerful texts that Tolstoy uses to support his philosophy of service is the so-called parable of the Final Judgement in the Gospel of Matthew. According to that parable, it is not possible to touch or see God, but it is possible to touch, see, and help our human brothers who are His manifestations and who are in need of our help. The King or Lord of that story insists that He was present under the guise of those who needed such help, and, that the most appropriate religious duty, or duty towards God, is to feed the hungry, give drink to the thirsty, clothe the naked, welcome in one's home the strangers, help and comfort the sick, the poor, and the prisoners.

Tolstoy's awareness of social needs and social issues led him to scrutinize the mechanism of institutional violence. In so doing, he listed some of the activities and professions most notorious in fostering a loveless or less than fully loving society. Those guilty in his eyes of fostering values of lovelessness and unauthentic living are those practicing the following behaviors:

- statesmen and political figures, to the extent that they partake in the functioning of the repressive mechanism of the state;

- all those engaged in the taking of lives through war, and those who aid and abet the activity of taking lives in war, such as soldiers, officers, and other military staff, including recruit trainers and all those involved in the manufacturing and sale of weapons;

- judges, lawyers, and others involved in the judiciary as we know it, to the extent that its functioning is a repressive mechanism;

- all the writers and artists who do not pursue the highest aims of art (these aims are viewed by Tolstoy as being: the conveying to others of some heartfelt experience or feeling in such a way as to forcefully impress that experience upon others, and the joining of humans together in the same feelings);

- academics and other teachers, to the extent that they do not know that they are to teach the highest values such as self-improvement, care and concern for each other, commitment to the well-being of others, and altruism;

- scientists, to the extent that they gather superficial, trivial, or futile information (merely serving the existing order) rather than information truly useful to humankind;

- priests, ministers, and theologians, to the extent that they view themselves as specialized, privileged intermediaries between humans and the spiritual experience;

- M. D. s and other medical staff, to the extent that they do not practice holistic and preventive medicine, and in some cases go to extremes of using extraordinary means to artificially extend life;

- those who participate in the oppression of the poor through their activity as money-lenders, usurers, or tax-collectors;

- all those of us, in any and every society, who practice violence, coercion, and oppression.

In Tolstoy's view, being engaged in the above-mentioned forms of behavior means leading an unquestioned life, that is, failing to question what he called *social deceits* or *deceits of culture* such as inauthentic education, art, government, law, science, or religion. Insofar as we do not question such social deceits, we consciously or unconsciously endorse them, and thus are guilty of endorsing lovelessness and violence. According to Tolstoy, denouncing deceits of culture as well as social injustice is a crucial part of the moral life. We are guilty of lovelessness and violence when we commit an injustice or unwittingly endorse injustice. Since times immemorial there has been a tendency in every society for the weak to be crushed with overwork while the strong are freed from even minimal manual work; the moral life requires that we become aware of that fact.

We practice lovelessness and violence whenever we exert pressure, coercion, and oppression upon others, whenever we exploit them. Lovelessness and violence are there whenever the economically stronger, the over-fed or well-fed, and the idle take advantage of the economically weaker, the hungry, and those crushed with overwork.

Tolstoy defined slavery as the situation in which "there is a person who does not labor because another is compelled to work for that person." He felt that, in that sense, slavery has continued into the twentieth century (Tolstoy, *The Slavery of Our Times*). Tolstoy considers that excessive wealth and idleness are the direct cause of excessive poverty and toil. He calls upon the rich to put an end to such a situation, to stop "sitting on the poor man's back" and using that poor man as a beast of burden; instead, he urges the rich to "get off the poor's backs."

The positive behavior that according to Tolstoy must replace lovelessness and violence is universal love and non-violence. To implement such behavior, Tolstoy urges us to:

a) Become aware of the plight of the downtrodden and the have-nots.

b) Denounce the deceits of culture, and denounce social injustice.

c) Renounce our wills, our personal lives, our personal desires and happiness; and, by devoting ourselves to the well-being of humanity, find the true life, by obeying the will of the Higher Power which gave us life.

d) Feed the hungry, give drink to the thirsty, clothe the naked, help the poor and prisoners, provide for other basic needs. Serve others through our immediate, direct labor and involvement.

e) To the extent that it is possible, rather than make our life-work consist of "amusing the well-fed," make it focus on meeting the basic needs of those in greatest need.

f) Devote at least part of our time to the practice of *bread-labor*, which is a beneficent law of life, and should be viewed as a religious duty. For Tolstoy, bread-labor is to be understood as labor that provides food, drink, clothes, shelter, and fuel to the poorest and neediest. Such a practice will help correct the imbalance between the rich and the poor, will generally help us better understand the situation of the poor, and help the rich achieve some degree of solidarity with the poor.

g) Instead of living a consumeristic life, practice intentional simplicity and frugality. (This is a support strategy for point no. 6 above.)

Tolstoy's comprehensive investigation of the deceits of culture led him to embrace political theory (views on the state, government, law, and the military), socio-economic theory, social criticism, education, and aesthetics, in addition to philosophical and spiritual insights. There can be no deep acquaintance with Tolstoy's "spiritual" message while avoid-ing contact with his views on these various social issues, as presented systematically in the chapters of this book. Let the reader be warned: heeding Tolstoy's message may lead to a very thorough rearrangement and reorientation of our lives.

Tolstoy played the leading role in devising a new doc-trine—a well-integrated philosophy and strategy of nonvio-lence. While he based that philosophy on the precepts of the Buddha, Jesus, and the Taoist Way of Life, the credit goes to him for elaborating an integral doctrine of nonviolence in a form attuned to the modern context. Tolstoy's fourfold program for nonviolent social change—stressing the need for a nonviolent economy, nonviolent communication, non-violent government, and nonviolent education—has been retained by Mahatma Gandhi. *The Wisdom of Humankind* is a condensed statement of Tolstoy's program of universal love and nonviolence.

In conclusion, let it be said that in all essentials, the various points of Tolstoy's philosophy are identical with those that his disciple Mahatma Gandhi was to evolve. If one should judge a tree by its fruit, then surely our assessment of the achievement of Tolstoy the mentor and inspirer should take into consideration a crucial part of his legacy—the life-work and vast influence of Gandhi, his most prominent disciple.

That same inspiration is now being offered to the reader of *The Wisdom of Humankind.*

Terms and Key Words

Meanings of certain key words used in this book

Belief: A negative, uncritical attitude or form of mental behavior —as in the expressions, "false belief," "blind belief," "wrong belief." A failure to use our reason where it should be used. (See *Reason* entry, below.) The term is opposed to "faith" (see *Faith* entry).

Blessedness: See *Happiness* entry.

Excess: Excess or overabundance (in traditional English, "surfeit") leads to the fault of overindulgence.

Faith: A reasonable assumption; accepting "on faith" something which it makes sense to accept; right understanding of spiritual truths, and willingness to act on them. Faith is compatible with reason. As opposed to "belief" (see *Belief* entry), "faith" is a positive term.

Fault: The term used most frequently here in lieu of the more traditional Christian or Judaic term "sin." (See *Sin.*) A fault is a failure to do the will of the higher power and to do what is best for me. A fault may be set straight by practicing the appropriate kind of effort (see Chapters 20 through 27).

God: An invisible and eternal power that sustains the world, and keeps it going. Also sometimes referred to here as "the Spirit," and generally also known as "the Supreme Being," "the Cosmic Power," "higher principle," or "higher power that gives us life." (See Chapter 4, section 2; Chapter 26, section 1.)

Government: Strictly speaking, the Russian word (*gosudarstvo*) used by Tolstoy translates as "state." However, Tolstoy in places uses the term where in English we would say, "the government." He lists "the authorities," "the State," and "the government" as the definitions of that unclear and not very precise "they" to whom many citizens feel they owe blind obedience or allegiance.

Happiness: The dictionary meaning for the word used by Tolstoy is also "blessedness." Here this word is usually rendered as "happiness," and sometimes as "blessedness," "blessing," and "well-being."

Kingdom of Heaven: A term from the New Testament. Also called "Kingdom of God," or "Spiritual Kingdom." Rather than any earthly regime, the term means: the reign or dominion of God that is brought about by our acceptance of God's will for us, by our acknowledgement of the fatherhood of God, and by our experiencing brotherly/sisterly feelings toward all in the human family.

Neighbor: The person next to me, the person I am in contact with, under whatever circumstances. Tolstoy (followed in this by Mahatma Gandhi) went in the direction of viewing *all* members of the human family as neighbors.

Rational: Based on reason, compatible with reason, verified by reason, acceptable to reason. Tolstoy felt reason is a higher faculty which is not at odds with Love, but rather makes us more attuned to love. Rational people are people who use their reason and understanding, and who are thinking and reasoning people. (See Chapter 27, Section 5.) Tolstoy maintains that there is a rational clarity to the Gospel which agrees with natural truth and with the light of reason in us.

Reason: A higher faculty (ability) in each of us. It is compatible with higher Love, and even reinforces Love. (See Chapter 1, Section 8 about the reason-faith relationship.)

Sexual restraint: The term most often used here in lieu of "chastity."

Sexual unrestraint: The term most often used here in lieu of "lustfulness."

Sin: A traditional term in the Judaic and Christian traditions, which now carries an overlay of guilt to many. In one place, Tolstoy himself defines "sins" as "mistakes, false actions." In this English edition the term "fault" is usually used in lieu of "sin." (See *Fault.*)

Soul: Also referred to as "the spirit" or "the spirit within," that is, within each of us.

State, the: See *Government.*

Superstition: a blind or irrational (unreasonable) belief, one not supported by reason; a distortion of thought; a distortion of the thinking process, and of rational thinking; an unexamined attitude; an empty, dead, or crystallized acceptance handed over from an earlier time when that acceptance made sense; a mechanical acceptance of a partial truth which no longer makes sense; blind belief in an ancient tradition that has never been seriously examined. Close in meaning to "unquestioned myth." (See Chapter 6; Chapter 27, Sections 1 and 3.)

Suggested Readings

Attar, Farid al-Din. *Muslim Saints and Mystics.* A. J. Araberry, transl. Boston: Routledge & Kegan Paul, 1973.

Aurobindo, Sri. *Essays on the Gita.* New York: Sri Aurobindo Library, 1950.

Aurobindo, Sri. *The Life Divine.* New York: Sri Aurobindo Library, 1949.

Bhagavad Gita, The. Juan Mascaró, trsl. New York: Viking Penguin, 1973.

Bloom, Harold. *The Western Canon: The Books and School of the Ages.* New York: Harcourt Brace, 1994.

Buber, Martin. *Tales of the Hasidim: Early Masters.* New York: Schocken, 1948.

Bucke, Richard M. *Cosmic Consciousness.* Secaucus, N. J. : Citadel, 1970.

Buddhist Bible, A. Dwight Goddard, ed. Boston: Beacon, 1970.

Bunyan, John. *Pilgrim's Progress.* New York: Dutton, 1970.

Caussade, Jean-Pierre de. *The Sacrament of the Present Moment.* Kitty Muggeridge, transl. San Francisco: Harper & Row, 1982.

Chesterton, G. K. *St. Francis of Assisi.* Garden City, NY: Doubleday, 1957.

Cloud of Unknowing, The. Ira Progoff, transl. New York: Dell, 1957.

Confucius. *The Wisdom of Confucius.* Lin Yutang, transl. & ed. New York: Modern Library, 1948.

Dalai Lama of Tibet, The Fourteenth. *Kindness, Clarity, and Insight.* Jeffrey Hopkins, transl. & ed. Ithaca, NY: Snow Lion, 1984.

Dalai Lama of Tibet, The Fourteenth. *Ocean of Wisdom: Guidelines for Living.* Santa Fe, NM: Clear Light Publishers, 1989.

Dhammapada, The. Juan Mascaro, transl. Baltimore, MD: Penguin, 1973.

Donskov, Andrew and John Woodsworth, eds. *Lev Tolstoy and the Concept of Brotherhood.* Ottawa: Legas, 1996.

Emerson, Ralph Waldo. *Essays.*

Epictetus. *The Manual* (*Enchiridion*).

Essential Gandhi, The. Louis Fischer, ed. New York: Random House, 1962.

Fedotov, George P. , comp. & ed. *A Treasury of Russian Spirituality.* Belmont, MA: Nordland, 1975.

Fischer, Louis. *The Life of Mahatma Gandhi.* New York: Macmillan, 1962.

Foster, Richard J. *Celebration of Discipline: The Path to Spiritual Growth.* San Francisco: Harper San Francisco, 1988. (Contains a useful annotated list of suggested readings.)

Gandhi, M. K. *All Men Are Brothers.* New York: UNESCO World Without War Publications, 1958.

Gandhi, M. K. *An Autobiography: The Story of my Experiments with Truth.* Boston: Beacon, 1972.

Gandhi, M. K. *Non-Violent Resistance.* Bharatan Kumarappa, transl. New York: Schocken, 1961.

Gustafson, Richard E. *Leo Tolstoy: Resident and Stranger.* Princeton, NJ: Princeton University Press, 1983.

Heard, Gerald. *A Preface to Prayer.* New York: Harper, 1944.

Huxley, Aldous. *The Perennial Philosophy.* New York: Harper & Row, 1970.

James, William. *The Varieties of Religious Experience.* New York: New American Library, 1958.

John of the Cross, St. *Dark Night of the Soul.* E. Allison Peers, transl. Garden City, NY: Doubleday, 1959.

Jones, Cheslyn, Geoffrey Wainwright, & Edward Yarnold, eds. *The Study of Spirituality: An Historical Sketch.* Chicago: Loyola University Press, 1984.

Jung, Carl G. *Psychology and Religion: West and East.* New Haven: Yale University Press, 1938.

Kenworthy, Leonard S. *Think on These Things: An Anthology of Inspirational Quotations.* Grand Rapids, Michigan: Four Corners Press, 1987.

Keyes, Ken, Jr. *Handbook to Higher Consciousness.* Coos Bay, Oregon: Love Line Books, 1985.

Koran (Qur'an), The. Transl. N. J. Dawood. New York: Penguin, 1981.

Lao Tzu. *The Way of Life: A New Translation of the Tao Te Ching.* R. B. Blakney, transl. New York: New American Library, 1955.

Leckey, Dolores R. *The Ordinary Way: A Family Spirituality.* New York: Crossroad, 1982.

Lewis, C. S. *Mere Christianity.* New York: Macmillan, 1973.

Life of Milarepa: Tibet's Great Yogi. W. Y. Evans-Wentz, transl. New York: Paragon, 1972.

Lourié, Yakov Solomonovich. *Posle Lva Tolstogo (After Leo Tolstoy).* St. Petersburg: Dmitrii Bulanin, 1993. (English translation forthcoming.)

Maharshi, Ramana. *The Spiritual Teaching of Ramana Maharshi.* Introduction by Carl Jung. Berkeley, CA: Shambala, 1972.

Marcus Aurelius. *The Meditations of Marcus Aurelius.* George Long, transl. New York: Avon, 1993.

Merton, Thomas. *A Thomas Merton Reader.* Thomas P. McDonnell, ed. Garden City, NY: Doubleday, 1974.

Nhat Hanh, Thich. *The Miracle of Mindfulness!: A Manual on Meditation.* Boston: Beacon Press, 1976.

Nigosian, Solomon. *Islam: The Way of Submission.* London: Crucible, 1987.

Orwin, Donna Tussing. *Tolstoy's Thought and Art.* Princeton, NJ: Princeton University Press, 1993.

Osborne, Arthur. *Ramana Maharshi and the Path to Self-Knowledge.* New York: Weiser, 1954.

Osborne, Arthur. *The Teachings of Ramana Maharshi.* New York: Random House, 1971.

Ouspensky, P. D. *The Fourth Way.* New York: Random House, 1971.

Ouspensky, P. D. *The Psychology of Man's Possible Evolution.* New York: Random House, 1974.

Patanjali. *How to Know God: The Yoga Aphorisms of Patanjali.* Swami Prabhavananda & Christopher Isherwood, transl. New York: New American Library, 1953.

Peck, M. Scott. *Meditations from the Road: Daily Reflections from The Road Less Traveled* and *The Different Drum.* New York: Simon & Schuster, 1993.

Pennington, M. Basil, Alan Jones, & Mark Booth, eds. *The Living Testament: The Essential Writings of Christianity Since the Bible.* San Francisco: Harper & Row, 1985.

Phillips, Dorothy Berkley, ed. *The Choice is Always Ours: An Anthology on the Religious Way.* Wheaton, Illinois: Theosophical Publishing House, 1977.

Pilgrim, The. *The Way of a Pilgrim and The Pilgrim Continues his Way.* R. M. French, transl. New York: Ballantine, 1979.

Powers, Thomas E. *Invitation to a Great Experiment: Exploring the Possi-*

bility that God can Be Known. Garden City, N. Y. : Doubleday, 1979. (Contains a useful list of suggested readings.)

Rahula, Walpola. *What the Buddha Taught.* New York: Grove Press, rev. ed., 1977.

Ramakrishna, Sri. *The Gospel of Sri Ramakrishna.* Swami Nikhilananda, transl. New York: Ramakrishna-Vivekananda Center, 1969.

Rumi, Jaladu'ddin. *The Mathnawi.* 5 vols. Reynold A. Nicholson, transl. London: Luzac, 1926.

Schuon, Frithjof. *The Transcendent Unity of Religions.* New York: Pantheon, 1953.

Schuon, Frithjof. *Understanding Islam.* New York: Penguin, 1972.

Schweitzer, Albert. *Thoughts for our Times.* Erica Anderson, ed. New York: The Pilgrim Press, 1975.

Scupoli, Dom Lorenzo. *The Spiritual Combat & A Treatise on Peace of Soul.* William Lester & Robert Mohan, transl. TAN Books & Publishers, 1990.

Sen, K. M. *Hinduism.* New York: Penguin,1976.

Shankara. *The Crest-Jewel of Discrimination.* Swami Prabhavananda & Christopher Isherwood, transl. Hollywood, CA: Vedanta Press, 1978.

Suzuki, Shunryu. *Zen Mind, Beginner's Mind.* Trudy Dixon, ed. New York: Weatherhill, 1976.

Suzuki, D. T. *The Essence of Buddhism.* London: Buddhist Society, 1947.

Suzuki, D. T. *Introduction to Zen Buddhism.* New York: Grove Press, 1964.

Teresa of Avila, St. *The Interior Castle.* E. Allison Peers, transl. Garden City, NY: Doubleday, 1961.

Thomas a Kempis. *The Imitation of Christ.* Garden City, NY: Doubleday, 1968.

Tolstoy, Leo. *A Confession.*

Tolstoy, Leo. *Anna Karenina. Critical Edition,* George Gibian, ed. New York: Norton, 1970.

Tolstoy, Leo. *The Kingdom of God is Within You: Christianity not as a Mystic Religion but as a new Theory of Life.* Lincoln, Nebraska: University of Nebraska Press, 1984.

Tolstoy, Leo. *The Law of Love and the Law of Violence.* Santa Barbara, CA: Concord Grove Press, 1981.

Tolstoy, Leo. *Why Do Men Stupefy Themselves?* Hankins, NY: East Ridge Press, 1975. (Contains three essays by Tolstoy, including the all-important "Industry and Idleness.")

Tozer, A. W. *The Knowledge of the Holy.* New York: Harper & Bros., 1961.

Tulasidas. *The Ramayana of Tulasidasa.* Gorakhpur, India: Gita Press, 1976.

Ugolino di Monte Santa Maria, Brother. *The Little Flowers of St. Francis.* Garden City, NY: Doubleday, 1958.

Underhill, Evelyn. *Mysticism.* New York: Dutton, 1961.

Underhill, Evelyn. *Practical Mysticism.* New York: World, Meridian Books, 1955.

Universal House of Justice. *To the Peoples of the World: A Baha'i Statement on Peace.* Ottawa: Association for Baha'i Studies, 1986.

Vasto, Lanza del. *Principles and Precepts of the Return to the Obvious.* New York: Schocken Books, 1974.

Vedanta for the Western World. Christopher Isherwood, ed. Hollywood, CA: Vedanta Press, 1945.

Vitray-Meyerovitch, Eva de. *Rumi and Sufism.* Sausalito, CA: Post-Apollo Press, 1989.

Ware, Timothy, ed. *The Art of Prayer: An Orthodox Anthology.* London: Faber & Faber, 1966.

Watts, Alan. *The Way of Zen.* New York: Random House, 1974.

Wilson, Andrew. *World Scripture: A Comparative Anthology of Sacred Texts.* New York: Paragon House, 1993.

Writings from the Philokalia on the Prayer of the Heart. E. Kadloubovsky & G. E. H. Palmer, transl. London: Faber, 1951.

Yutang, Lin. *Wisdom of China and India.* New York: Random House, 1942.

APPENDIX FOUR

Sources

Authors and Texts that Tolstoy Drew upon or Paraphrased

The following is a listing of the specific sources upon which Tolstoy drew in compiling *The Wisdom of Humankind*. He quotes both from the writings of individual authors (without title references, and without page references), and from Scriptures of different traditions (all without chapter or verse references). In addition, Tolstoy drew upon numerous almanacs and miscellanies or general collections of folk wisdom, proverbs, and sayings of sages and philosophers. These sources are usually not acknowledged by him; instead, Tolstoy provides a paraphrase of passages from these sources without identifying the sources.

Following current usage, dates are given as follows:

B.C.E. (Before the Current Era)— in lieu of B.C.

C.E. (Current Era)—in lieu of A.D.

The traditional abbreviation "ca" (Latin *circa*, approximately) is given for those dates which are approximate.

Amiel, Henri-Frédéric (1821-1881). Swiss-French writer, poet, and moralist. Author of *Fragments of an Intimate Diary*, now recognized as one of the most important documents in modern introspective literature. Elsewhere Tolstoy commented, "[. . . it seems to Amiel,] as is characteristic of one who honestly seeks the truth, that the more he knows the more he needs to know . . . and then he is constantly conscious of his ignorance. [. . . Amiel's *Diary*] is full of life, vigor, instruction, consolation, and will always remain one of the best books, such as have been unwittingly left to us by men like Marcus Aurelius, Pascal, and Epictetus."

Angelus Silesius (1624-1677). German Catholic mystic poet and polemicist. His most notable works are collections of poems entitled *The Cherubic Wanderer* and *Holy Joy of the Soul*. These works reflect important aspects of Christian spirituality and had a great influence on both Catholic and Protestant authors. According to Angelus, humans must empty and surrender themselves totally in order to become their true nature—an eternal reflection of the divine. He was staunchly opposed to Protestantism, which he attacked in numerous polemical pieces.

Arkhangelskii, Aleksandr Ivanovich (1857-1906). Assistant veterinarian. Author of the book *Whom Should We Serve?*, which was held in high esteem by Tolstoy.

Bakunin, Mikhail Aleksandrovich (1814-1876). Russian revolutionary and theoretician of anarchism. He actively participated in European revolutionary movements and was active within the First International. He presented his libertarian and anti-state views in his book *The State and Anarchy*. Such views exerted significant influence on the European workers' movement, and made him an opponent of Karl Marx.

Ballou, Adin (1803-1890). American writer, Universalist clergyman, reformer, and supporter of nonviolent resistance; founder of the Hopedale Community.

Basil, Saint (ca. 329-379 C.E.). Surnamed the Great, Bishop, one of the Cappadocian Fathers of the Christian Church, author of many remarkable sermons and organizer of oriental monasticism. He fostered monastic communities in which hard work and charitable service replaced the asceticism and isolation of hermits. Author of many significant religious works, including two influential *Monastic Rules*.

Baxter, Richard (1651-1691). English Puritan, theologian and author of over two hundred works including most notably *The Saint's Everlasting Rest* (1650), and *The Reformed Pastor* (1656), which influenced seventeenth-century English Protestantism. He functioned as peacemaker among clashing Protestant denominations.

Bentham, Jeremy (1748-1832). English economist, political theorist, philosopher, and moralist. An advocate of utilitarianism (the doctrine that the purpose of all action should be to bring about the greatest happiness to the greatest number) and an early father of the welfare state, he believed that the aim of government should be "the greatest good of the greatest number." Author of several works on law, politics, and morals.

Bhagavad Gita, The ("The Song of God"). A lengthy spiritual poem written between the 1st and 2nd centuries C.E., which contains a dialogue between the god Krishna and the Indian hero Arjuna on human nature and human purpose. In the book, Krishna outlines the path of devotion to God (or *Bhakti*), and emphasizes the need for humans to perform the duties of their caste selflessly. It is the leading religious text of the predominant Vaisnava Bhakti (devotional) sect, and the most popular text in Hinduism.

Bondarev, Timofei Mikhailovich (1820-1898). Self-taught peasant from the Don region, author of the composition *Industriousness and Parasitism*, or the *Triumph of the Farmer*. In his own essay, "Industry and Idleness," Tolstoy fully endorsed Bondarev's views.

Book of Manu, The (2nd-1st cent. B.C.E.). An ancient Hindu treatise in twelve chapters on civil and religious duties, and the oldest known book on Hindu Law. According to Hindu mythology, Manu was the father of the human race and the first law-giver. The book sets out the legendary origins of the various Hindu castes, and describes in detail their rights and duties. In its treatment the text does not distinguish between religious law and practices and secular law. It exerted monumental influence on Indian society, and provided caste Hindus with a system of practical morality.

Browne, Edward Harold (1811-1891). English religious writer, professor of divinity at Cambridge, England, then bishop.

Buddha (the Enlightened One; 563-483 B.C.E.). The name given to the founder of Buddhism, an Indian prince, originally named Siddhartha Gautama. After years of solitary contemplation, he began to teach a doctrine of self-denial and universal brotherhood. Buddhism emphasizes physical and spiritual discipline as a means of liberation from the physical world. The goal for the Buddhist is to attain Nirvana, a state of complete peace in which one is free from the distractions of desire. Buddhism originated in India, but has followers throughout the world, most notably in East and Southeast Asia.

Carlyle, Thomas (1795–1881). English philosopher, essayist, and historian. He was influenced by Calvinism and by such German thinkers as Goethe and Kant. He won fame as a historian (*The French Revolution*), as a popular lecturer (*Heroes and Hero Worship* and *Past and Present*), and as a biographer of Frederick the Great. An enemy of 19th century rationalism and materialism and mass industrial democracy, he was a practitioner of philosophical idealism. He was known as the Sage of Chelsea, admired by Emerson, John Stuart Mill, Ruskin, and Dickens, who dedicated *Hard Times* to him. He was the author of the book *The Riddle of the Sphinx*, of which a translation was published in Moscow in 1900.

Carpenter, Edward (1844–1929). English poet and prose-writer. He was a pioneer of the "simple life" movement and identified with the anti-industrial arts and crafts movement of his day. His chief works include *The Art of Creation* (1904), *Towards Democracy* (1905), and *Love's Coming of Age* (1906). He was influenced by Walt Whitman whom he met on a visit to the United States in 1877. As a Socialist, he was a follower of William Morris and more interested in social reform through return to rural crafts than in political revolution. He had a lifelong interest in music, and composed the well-known labor song "England Arise."

Cato, Marcus Porcius (234-149 B.C.E.). Otherwise known as Cato the Elder or Cato the Censor; a Roman statesman, orator, and writer known as an inflexible champion of the moral virtues of the early Republic. He was also known for his insistence that Carthage was Rome's permanent enemy, and for his conservative and anti-Hellenic policies. Author of a history of Rome and a treatise on agriculture.

Channing, William Ellery (1780-1842). American clergyman and writer, who was a leader and organizer of the Unitarian movement in New England. An opponent of slavery, he achieved eminence as a philosopher, theologian, preacher, and philanthropist. He spoke for humanitarianism and tolerance, in contrast to the dogmatism of the Calvinists. His liberal views on religion and morality had a profound influence on many writers including Emerson and Oliver Wendell Holmes.

Chelcicky, Petr (ca. 1390-ca. 1460). Czech religious and political writer, author of *The Net of Faith*. As summed up by Tolstoy, his fundamental idea is that "Christianity, by allying itself with temporal power in the days of Constantine . . . has become completely distorted, and has ceased to be Christian altogether. . . . Christianity, expecting from its followers gentleness, meekness, peaceableness, forgiveness of injuries, turning the other cheek when one is struck, and love for enemies, is inconsistent with the use of force, which is an indispensable condition of authority."

Chernyshevsky, Nikolai Gavrilovich (1828-1889). Russian literary critic and political thinker (positive materialist and socialist). Leader of the radical intelligentsia, and an important early member of the revolutionary movement in Russia. In his view, art is a reproduction of reality, and therefore inferior to it; literature is justified only if it promotes social progress, and serves a progressive social tendency. As a socialist, he considered that the complete reorganization of economic institutions was necessary for progress. His ethical views were utilitarian.

Chrysostom, Saint John ("the Golden-Mouthed Orator;" ca. 345-407 C.E.). Greek writer, patriarch of Constantinople and Doctor of the Christian Church, whose writings mark him as one of the most distinguished of Christian theologians. His eloquence was outstanding. Some of his famed sermons contain scathing attacks against the rich for not heeding the poverty surrounding them. He felt that salvation can only be collective, and that true perfection consists in forgetting of self while serving others.

Cicero, Marcus Tullius (106-43 B.C.E.). Statesman, author, and the most famous Roman orator. His many speeches to the Roman Senate are famous for their rhetorical techniques and their ornate style. Of his speeches, fifty-eight survive. They include orations in both civil and criminal cases, speeches to the Senate, and harangues to the people.

Cleobulus (6th cent. B.C.E.). A Greek ruler, poet, and riddlemaker. He was known as one of the seven Greek Sages and tyrant of Lindus on the island of Rhodes. He is credited with the maxim, "Moderation is the chief good." He may have been the first to put riddles into verse.

Clifford, John (1836-1923). English Baptist clergyman and an active member of the radical wing of the Liberal Party. As a social reformer he organized the passive resistance movement against the English Education Act of 1902, which required public funds to support denominational schools. He was the first president of the Baptist World Alliance, 1905-1911.

Combe, Abraham (1785-1827). Scottish socialist philosopher and ardent disciple of Robert Owen. He was the founder of several communistic communities. One noted book by him was *The Religious Creed of the New Systems.*

Confucius (551-479 B.C.E.). Chinese philosopher and sage. His teachings, which stress following traditional ways, have come down as a collection of short sayings. Confucianism is a system of ethics, founded on the teachings of Confucius, that influenced the traditional culture of China. Confucianism places a high value on learning, and stresses family and natural relationships.

Considérant, Victor Prosper (1808-1893). French Utopian socialist who devoted himself to advancing Charles Fourier's Utopianism. After Fourier's death in 1837 Considérant became the acknowledged leader of the communitarian Socialists and took charge of *La Phalange*, the theoretical organ of Fourieriest Utopianism. He sought a reorganized society, providing everyone with suitable work —"the right to work"—and adequate reward through rationally structured communities named phalansteries. During his second visit to the United States, Considérant founded the short-lived communistic colony of La Réunion (1855-57) near Dallas, Texas. After spending twenty years in exile in the United States, he returned to France in 1869 and wrote in support of pacifism.

Crosby, Ernest Howard (1856-1907). American writer, close to Tolstoy's views.

Demophilus. Greek Pythagorean philosopher.

Dhammapada, The (3rd century B.C.E.). A collection of sayings by Siddhartha Gautama, the Buddha. One of the most ancient and venerated monuments of Buddhist literature, this collection deals with the treading of the Path of Perfection, which leads to nirvana—the state of enlightenment or liberation, when desires or cravings are extinguished, and the ego is dissolved. This text urges us to pursue spiritual development now, and describes the true joys of spiritual fulfillment in comparison with passing pleasures.

Dostoevsky, Fiodor Mikhailovich (1821-1881). Russian author, one of the world's outstanding novelists. His most famous novels were *Crime and Punishment* (which we know for sure was read by Tolstoy), *The Possessed,* and *The Brothers Karamazov.* He was the father of the modern psychological novel; as such, he provided many brilliant insights into extremes of human nature. He was a strong opponent of atheistic humanism, while professing his own original brand of "soil-bound" ideology—national, democratic, and Russian Orthodox Christian. Perhaps best known for his treatment of the problems of human freedom and the destiny of humankind.

Eliot, George (1819-1881). Pseudonym of the English Romantic novelist Mary Ann Evans. A scholarly intellectual and friend of Herbert Spencer, she turned to fiction in her late thirties and joined the ranks of the foremost English novelists with *Adam Bede, Middlemarch, The Mill on the Floss,* and *Silas Marner,* all realistic portrayals of rural, middle-class English life.

Emerson, Ralph Waldo (1803-1882). American poet, lecturer, essayist, and a leading member of the New England idealists known as the Transcendentalists, who advised people to look for God-given power within themselves. In his essay, "Self-Reliance," and in other works, Emerson stressed the importance of the individual and encouraged people to rely on their own intuitive judgement. Many in the nineteenth century took inspiration from Emerson, especially through his brief and pointed sayings and urgings, such as "Hitch your wagon on to a star."

Epictetus (ca. 50-ca. 135 C.E.). Greek philosopher and the great spokesman for the Stoic school of philosophy. In his sayings (compiled as the texts *Dissertations* and the *Manual*), he views humans as responsible members of society, and as citizens with an interest in their own welfare, as well as in the common welfare. He stresses that by the act of will we can attain great moral stature, and achieve self-mastery, while contributing to a better life for others.

Erasmus, Desiderius (1469-1536). Dutch Catholic reformer, writer on the Church Fathers, classical scholar, and the greatest of the Renaissance humanists. He attempted to solve some of the controversies of the time of the Reformation. Erasmus urged changes in Christian practice, including more piety, reforms that would make the Catholic Church less worldly, and the study of the literature of ancient Greece and Rome. His most famous work is the satire *The Praise of Folly*.

Fénelon, François de Salignac de la Mothe (1651-1715). French Catholic Archbishop, religious activist, educator, and mystical theologian, whose works had a strong impact on educational philosophy, on literature, and on political theory. He was the author of *Fables*, of other educational writings, and of religious-polemical writings. He advocated a quietistic form of spirituality.

Flammarion, Camille (1842-1925). French astronomer and popularizer of science.

Francis of Assisi, Saint (1182-1226). An Italian saint of the Christian Church, mystic, and founder of the Order of Franciscans. He is known for his simplicity, devotion to poverty, and love of nature. Tolstoy much admired his humility.

Frederick the Great (1712-1786). King of Prussia.

Geikie, John Cunningham (1824-1906). Scottish religious writer and minister. His writings had appeal for their historical and practical (rather than purely theological) references and significance. His popular ten-volume *Hours with the Bible*, or *The Scripture in the Light of Modern Discovery and Knowledge* may well have influenced Tolstoy's devising of the format of *The Wisdom of Humankind*.

George, Henry (1839-1897). American journalist, economist, and social reformer. His widely-circulated and influential book *Progress and Poverty* (1879) perhaps contributed more to interest in economics than any other single book. His central idea was to confront humankind with a dramatic and well reasoned exposure of the need to abolish the poverty and social injustice arising from land monopoly. He defended the Single Tax on land, and proposed abolishing all other taxes.

Giusti, Giuseppe (1809-1850). Italian poet and satirist, who attacked corruption and apathy among his own fellow countrymen, while denouncing Austrian control of Italy.

Goethe, Johann-Wolfgang von (1749-1832). Many-faceted German writer, most widely known for his poetic masterpiece *Faust*; also prominent as a statesman. Along with his remarkable achievements in such spheres as poetry, the novel, the philosophical essay, and scientific papers, he sought to foster cultural internationalism through a universal literature. His pantheism influenced the 19th-century German romantic movement.

Gogol, Nikolai Vasilevich (1809-1852). One of Russia's greatest writers, of Ukrainian background. He exposed the injustices of Russian life in writings that were seen by some as instruments of social change. For decades Soviet criticism propounded the notion that he was the founder of the Russian school of literary realism. The truth is that alongside realism and social criticism we find in him non-realism or a visionary vein, mysticism, and political conservatism. Thus, in 1847 he published a collection of moralizing statements endorsing serfdom and supporting such conservative bulwarks as autocracy and the Russian Orthodox establishment; in that book he emphasized that rather than theory or ideology, practical performance alone would improve Russian life. His most famous works are: the play *The Inspector General*, the story "The Overcoat," and his masterpiece, the novel *Dead Souls*, whose characters are spiritually dead. These characters are all caricatures and personifications of individual vices and have become types in Russian literature.

Grant, Allen (1848-1899). English novelist and Darwinist.

Heine, Heinrich (1797-1856). German romantic poet who sung brokenhearted pain with great poignancy. Political inspiration or desperate irony color many of his lyrics. His political-satirical statements brought him into conflict with German censorship. After he was relocated in France, he functioned as a bridge between German and French culture.

Heraclitus (ca. 530-470 B.C.E.). Greek philosopher who influenced Socrates, Plato, and Aristotle. He emphasized an underlying unity in the universe, and the capacity of all humans to attain universal reason. He saw the universe as in constant flux. He was the father of modern dialectics, as he believed that "war (that is, the clash of contradictory principles) is the father of all things."

Hertzen (also: Herzen, Gertsen), **Aleksandr Ivanovich** (1812-1870). Leading Russian humanist and socialist revolutionary thinker. One of the founders of Russian Populism (based on the belief that the Russian tradition of peasant communes could help the country attain socialism by means of a peasant revolution). An *émigré* from 1847, he published *The Bell*, the first Russian *émigré* journal, which had profound influence inside Russia. As a liberal socialist, Hertzen rejected the notion that human beings could or should be sacrificed for the sake of any abstract principle. Hertzen was critical of both

Tsarism and the Church, but also of capitalism, and argued for a socialist Russia.

Hitopadesha. Moralistic fables and proverbs composed in Sanskrit between the 10th and 14th centuries in Bengal, India.

Humboldt, Friedrich Wilhelm von (1767-1835). Prominent German diplomat, physiologist, and linguist who was the first to consider the interaction of culture, history, and anthropology with language, asserting that man's perception of the world is profoundly affected by language. He served as Prussia's ambassador to Vienna and London before resigning to protest his government's reactionary policies.

Hus, Jan (ca. 1370-1415). Czech Catholic priest, professor and Rector (Head) of Prague University. Denouncing the lax life of the clergy, he was involved in religious reform, as well as in the cause of Czech patriotism. Condemned by the Catholic Church on the charge of heresy, he was burned at the stake.

Jefferson, Thomas (1743-1826). Statesman, humanist, and revolutionary who became third president of the United States (1801-1809). He was a supporter of political and religious freedoms, and was entrusted with composing the American Declaration of Independence.

John the Evangelist (or John the Theologian or the Divine; first century C.E.). An early disciple of Jesus, author of the Fourth Gospel, perhaps identical with the Apostle John, son of Zebedee.

Juvenal, Decimus Junius (ca. 60-ca. 140 C. E.). Roman poet and satirist known for his acid and biting wit, and for his graphic accounts of the Roman Empire's injustice and degeneracy.

Kant, Immanuel (1724-1804). German philosopher who made revolutionary contributions to western philosophy in such works as his *Critique of Pure Reason.* Here Kant synthesized Cartesian rationalism and Humean skeptical empiricism, which divided philosophy in his day. He argued that thought and experience, rationality and empiricism, both play a necessary role in our attaining knowledge, though limited to those things accessible to our sense experience. Kant held that human thought is determined by *a priori* categories of the mind, such as space, time, and causality. He believed that God, free will, and the immortality of the soul could not be proved, but should be taken for granted. Other important contributions by him are in the field of moral theory. His book *Religion within the Limits of Reason* exerted significant influence on Tolstoy.

Krishna. Avatar or incarnation of the Hindu god Vishnu.

Kropotkin, Prince Peter Alekseevich (1842-1921). Russian geographer and revolutionary, a leading theoretician of anarchism, and a leader of the anarchist political movement. Exiled by the Russian government, he spent about four decades in various west European countries. For him, law is the consequence of the tendency of human beings to oppress fellow humans; it is reinforced by violence. He provides evidence from the animal kingdom to prove that species which practice mutual aid multiply faster than others. Opposing all State power, he advocated the abolition of states, and of private property, and the transforming of humankind into a federation of mutual-aid communities. According to him, capitalism cannot achieve full productivity, for it aims at maximum profits instead of production for human needs. All persons, including intellectuals, should practice manual labor. Goods should be distributed according to individual needs.

La Boétie, Etienne de (1530-1563). French writer. Author of *Discourse on Voluntary Slavery*, an analysis of how ordinary simple people accept the bondage enforced by tyrants or other willful rulers, and how such simple people endorse and implement state-decreed repression. This work is also a plea against such bondage.

La Bruyère, Jean de (1645-1696). French satirist and moralist who in his *Caractères* critiqued French aristocracy, attacking its false social status, vanity, corruption, and empty conformity.

Lactantius (ca. 240-ca. 320). One of the Latin Fathers of the Christian Church. First he was a pagan teacher of rhetoric during Diocletian's reign, and later became a Christian writer and apologist active during the reign of Roman Emperor Constantine. Admired for his clear and concise style, he wrote seven volumes of *Divine Institutions*, defending Christianity against any who would attempt to defame it.

Lamartine, Alphonse de (1791-1869). French poet, historian, and leading figure in the French Romantic movement. As part of his political career he fought for social reforms to help the impoverished of his day.

La Mennais, Félicité Robert de (1782-1854). French religious activist and political author who advocated the right of peoples to free themselves from rule in conflict with Christian principles. He saw political freedom as the very essence of Christianity. He became increasingly pantheistic in his beliefs toward the end of his life. Father of Christian socialism.

Lao Tsu (6th-5th cent. B.C.E.). Believed to be the author of the *Tao Te Ching* (*The Way of Life*), which encourages personal and social harmony with the unity of nature. In keeping with that aim, the text urges avoidance of ambitions (which are in contradiction with the achievement of harmony), a simple lifestyle and the overcoming of force by yielding (exemplified by water). It is said that Lao Tsu wrote the *Tao* only at the insistence of the Keeper of the Gate; Lao Tsu had become disheartened with the perpetual unnecessary struggles of man and was seeking to leave the province and re-enter nature. The Keeper refused to permit Lao Tsu out until he had written down his philosophy, fearing it would be lost to humanity. Lao Tsu complied and was permitted through, leaving the Keeper with the *Tao Te Ching*.

Larroque, Patrice, (1801-1879). French philosopher and Rector (Head) of the Academy of Lyons, France.

Lavater, Johann Kasper (1741-1801). Swiss poet, theologian, and mystic. He was also active as a physiognomist (that is, he practiced the art of determining character or personal characteristics from the form or features of the face and the rest of the body). He was a widely sought spiritual advisor and personal friend of Goethe.

Lavelle, Emile-Louis-Victor (1822-1892). Belgian historian and economist.

Lessing, Gotthold Ephraim (1729-1781). Dramatist, critic, prose stylist and major figure in Germany's 18th century golden age of literature. His most famous work, *Nathan the Wise,* calls for religious tolerance, placing individual character over religious beliefs as the judge of human goodness and worth. He delighted in exposing hypocrisy and duplicity in his many critical pieces.

Lichtenberg, Georg Christoph (1742-1799). German physicist, satirical writer, and critic.

Luther, Martin (1483-1546). German Augustinian friar who, appalled by the corruption of the medieval Christian Church, became the catalyst for the splintering of Christendom. He led a religious reform effort—the Protestant Reformation—that brought an end to the unchallenged Church authority of the Middle Ages, and spurred the Counter-Reformation, an effort within the Roman Catholic Church to reform itself and address its corruptions.

Machiavelli, Nicolò di Bernardo (1469-1527). Italian statesman, political philosopher, and writer. He was the author of the famous treatise *The Prince.* As opposed to classical Greek philosophers, who stressed the ways to achieve the best possible political regime, he realistically takes as his point of departure the way people actually function. His theory denounces the pretensions religion and theology may have to control political matters. He endeavors to promote a new political order within which to rule means to direct human nature away from its natural wickedness, in order to render human beings better.

Maimonides (1135-1204). Jewish theologian, physician, and codifier of Jewish law and the most celebrated Jewish philosopher in the Middle Ages. He sought to reconcile Judaism with classical Greek philosophy, and to unify faith and reason. He is praised also for a monumental and lucid codification of Talmudic law.

Mallory, Lucy (1846-1918?). American writer and editor who did pioneering work educating black and mulatto children, at a time when color prejudice did not yet allow for such work. In 1886 she founded the magazine *The World's Advanced Thought*, to which Tolstoy and other thinkers worldwide subscribed.

Marcus Aurelius (121-180 C.E.). Roman emperor known as a successful general, a wise and patient ruler, and a Stoic philosopher. His introspective *Meditations (Reflections of the Roman Emperor Marcus Aurelius)*, written in Greek, has been one of the most influential books composed by a ruler. In it, he reveals himself without arrogance as an instrument used for a time by Providence to guide the Roman Empire towards its destiny of becoming part of a dimly perceived world order. The virtues he espoused were those usually regarded as Christian, but he saw Christianity as an emotional, intolerant, and disruptive sect, which sought the empire's protection while refusing or avoiding military service or other duties. Such persecution as he practiced was on civic, not religious grounds. His reign was looked back on by later Romans as a Golden Age.

Martineau, Harriet (1802-1876). English novelist and radical journalist whose portrayals of the poor and suffering advocated social and economic reforms. She later wrote articles calling for the abolition of slavery in the United States.

Mazzini, Giuseppe (1805-1872). Italian writer, patriot, and political agitator who fought for Italian unity and the liberation of dominated people throughout Europe. His subversive writings spread his ideas throughout Italy. His ideas, along with his Young Italy organization, educated many and inspired uprisings against reactionary government rule. He dreamed of an end to political oppression everywhere.

Mencius (Latinized form of **Meng-tzu** or **Meng K'o**; 372-289 B.C.E.). Classical Chinese Confucianist philosopher. He believed that humans are inherently good and have an innate sense of right and wrong which leads to moral action. In addition, he felt that people have a right to rebel if their ruler lacks ethical qualifications. He endeavored to spread his ideas through various warring kingdoms. With time he became disappointed by the extent to which conflicts kept prevailing. He has been influencing Chinese thought to this day.

Menedemus of Eretria (ca. 339-265 B.C.E.). Greek philosopher. He entered politics, but his opponents drove him into exile. His philosophy is *eristic*—i.e., one which stresses disputation in order to persuade an opponent (rather than seeking the joint exploration of truth).

Molinari, Gustave de (1819-1911). Belgian economist. First active as a homeopathic medical doctor, then as journalist and economist.

Montaigne, Michel Eyquem de (1533-1592). French writer and philosopher, originator of the personal essay as a new literary form. At age 38 he withdrew to a rural area, away from worldly concerns, to devote himself to a study of himself; the result was his landmark *Essays*. Gathering that the human soul holds much more *space* than any worldly activity, he undertook a patient and systematic process of self-exploration. That led him to ponder "the human condition" as a whole, and to evolve a better-motivated way of life.

Montesquieu, Charles-Louis de (1689-1755). French author. Best known for his books *Persian Letters*, an incisive and witty critique of French society, and *The Spirit of Laws*, in which he related political laws to constitutions, mores, religion, trade, climate, and soil.

More, Sir Thomas (1478-1535). Author and Lord Chancellor of England. After turning away from the priesthood and asceticism, he studied law vigorously. Some claim that his famous book *Utopia* is a vitriolic attack, disguised as fiction, on modern society and politics. In the work, Utopia is the name of a communist island where the philosophy is pure utilitarianism and where the immediate pleasure of each individual must be delayed. The work can be seen as foreshadowing the thoughts of modern socialist reformers. For a time, he was in favor of reforming the Church and felt that the changes should stem from within and not forcefully, from the outside.

Morrison, Davidson J. (1843-1916). English economist and moralist. Corresponded with Tolstoy.

Moses (13th century B.C.E.). Major leader and spiritual guide of the Jewish people. He led the Jews across the Red Sea on their way to the Promised Land, and was the intermediary through whom God conveyed the Ten Commandments. From the pages of the Bible he emerges as the true founder of Judaism. He is acknowledged by Jews, Muslims, and Christians as a major prophet.

Muhammad (also, **Mohammed**; ca. 570-632). Arabian prophet and founder of Islam. He spent the early part of his life as a merchant before experiencing a prophetic summons from God. He went on to initiate in Islam a social, cultural, and religious movement that continues to have a profound effect on the modern world.

Nazhivin, Ivan Fiodorovich (1874-1940). Russian novelist. In the 1900s he was influenced by Tolstoy's ethical teachings and wrote many popular didactic narratives.

Newton, Herbert—not identified.

Parker, Theodore (1810-1860). American Unitarian clergyman and social reformer, who gave great help to the antislavery cause. He was a leader in the committee of vigilance, received runaway slaves, fought against their surrender, and aided their escape. He presented his appeal for the abolition of slavery in *A Letter to the People of the United States Touching the Matter of Slavery*, which was published in 1848. Other notable works by him include *The Transient and Permanent in Christianity* and *A Discourse of Matters Pertaining to Religion*.

Pascal, Blaise (1623-1662). French mathematician, scientist, Christian thinker and moralist. He is famous for a collection of reflections known as *Pensées (Thoughts)*. Pascal came to believe that reason alone could not satisfy people's hopes and aspirations, and that religious faith was therefore necessary. He distrusted human reason unsupported by faith and revelation. One famous line of his, "the heart has its reasons which reason cannot know." Tolstoy quoted from a Russian translation of Pascal's *Thoughts* published in 1899.

Paul, Saint (1st century C.E.). Known as Paul of Tarsus, a Christian preacher and teacher and Apostle to the Gentiles. Along with the Apostle Peter, Paul was one of the foremost leaders of the early Christian Church. Paul, originally called Saul, was at first an enemy and persecutor of the early Christians. As he rode to Damascus one day, seeking to suppress the Christians there, a strong light from heaven blinded him and God spoke to him. After this experience, Saul became a Christian. Going by the Greek name Paul, he spent the rest of his life bringing the Gospel to the people of his land. The *New Testament* includes his many epistles (letters) to the early Christian communities.

Paulsen, Friedrich (1846-1908). Neo-Kantian German philosopher and educator. He felt that the soul is known by the act of will. By "will" he meant neither rational desire, unconscious irrational will, nor conscious intelligent will, but an instinct, a "will to live." His ethics combined utilitarian and idealistic considerations.

Plato (427-347 B.C.E.). Greek philosopher, often considered the most important figure in Western philosophy. Plato was a student of Socrates, and later became a teacher of Aristotle. He founded a school in Athens called the Academy. Most of his writings are dialogues. He is best known for his theory that ideal forms or ideas, such as truth and good, exist in a realm beyond the material world. His chief subjects are ethics and politics. His best-known dialogues are: *The Republic,* which concerns the just state; the *Symposium,* which concerns the nature of love; and *Phaedo,* which deals with the immortality of the soul.

Plutarch (ca. 50-ca. 125). Prominent Greek writer and historian who is best known for a collection of over 60 *Lives* or *Parallel Lives* of famous Greek and Roman individuals. It was essentially as a philosopher and a moralist that Plutarch considered the lives of great persons; in this pursuit his primary interest was to discover the moral qualities of his subjects, to measure the extent of their influence, and assess their intellectual capacities. As a thinker Plutarch drew his inspiration from Platonism.

Proudhon, Pierre-Joseph (1809-1865). French theoretician of socialism. His book *What is Property?* (1840) propounds individualism colored with anarchism, and claims that "property is theft." He considered that only by doing away with capitalistic profit could humankind put an end to social injustice. The social revolution propounded by him was meant to preserve both the equality and the full freedom of individuals. For a while Proudhon polemicized with Karl Marx. In his key book, *Of Justice in Revolution and in the Church,* he opposed the religion of labor to the Christian religion.

Puisieux, Madeleine d'Arsant de (1720-1798). French moralist, novelist and radical social critic. She authored a plan for extending education to all classes. Some of her novels deal with the social education required for young women and men. Other works convey critiques of relationships between the sexes, the rights of individuals, religious intolerance, and the court and the nobility.

Pythagoras (ca. 580 B.C.E.-ca. 500 B.C.E.). Greek mathematician and philosopher. He felt that numbers are the principles, the source, and the roots of all things, including music.

Ramakrishna Paramahansa (1835-1886). One of the most revered saints of modern India. He was a Hindu mystic, who was influenced by the devotional school within Hinduism (*Bhakti*). He believed that mystical experience was the highest goal of all true religion. He stated that all religions which led to this goal were true, no matter how much their individual beliefs differed. He lived for some time as both a Christian and a Muslim. His thinking has remained influential up to the present day.

Rod, Edouard (1857-1910). French-speaking Swiss novelist. He was influenced by Schopenhauer. At first he was a realist-naturalist; thereafter he practiced psychological analysis. Also was politically active.

Rousseau, Jean-Jacques (1712-1778). French philosopher, one of the leading figures of the Enlightenment. He held that, in the state of nature, people are good, but that they are corrupted by social institutions; this notion became a central idea of Romanticism. Some of Rousseau's best-known writings are *The Social Contract*, an important influence on the French Revolution; *Emile*, a statement of his views on education; and his autobiography, *Confessions*.

Ruskin, John (1819-1900). English writer and art critic. Disturbed by the rapid spread of industrialization, he also wrote studies in morality: *Unto This Last, Sesame and Lilies*, and *The Crown of Wild Olive*.

Sadi (ca. 1184 or 1194-1282). Persian Sufi poet, one of the most celebrated and popular poets of his country. He wrote moralistic and epigrammatic prose on the ways of dervishes and kings, and lyrical poetry of beauty and warmth. Goethe, Emerson, and Thoreau were among his admirers. His best known works are *Bustan (Garden of Fruits)* and *Gulistan (Rosegarden)*. A famous remark by him is: "Conclude not that there is a fire in the hovel of thy indigent neighbor, the smoke that thou seest issuing from the chimney is the sign of his heart."

Said-Ben-Akhmed (died in 864). Spanish-language writer, born in Malaga. He wrote a *Description of Diverse Nations*.

Salter, Samuel (1710-1778). An extemporaneous English preacher who had several of his sermons published. He was a classical scholar and was also versed in modern literature.

Schopenhauer, Arthur (1788-1860). German philosopher. His major work, *The World as Will and Idea*, identified the unknowable reality of Kant as a blind will to live, animating all nature. He was influenced by Buddhism, and advocated the pursuit of activities, such as art and music, that tend to neutralize the will to live.

Scripture World Scriptures such as: the Christian *Bible;* the Jewish *Talmud;* the Muslim *Koran (Qur'an);* Hindu scriptures such as the *Bhagavad Gita* and the epic poems *Puranas* and *Kural;* Buddhist scriptures such as the *Dhammapada* and various *Suttras;* the Baha'i scriptures.

Seneca, Lucius Annaeus (4 B.C.E.-65 B.C.E.) Roman statesman, stoic philosopher, and dramatist, tutor and advisor to Nero and for a few years, virtual ruler of the Roman Empire. He amassed a great fortune and retired at 65 to write moral essays in a highly rhetorical style and nine tragic dramas in verse, which were greatly admired during the Renaissance.

Skovoroda, Grigorii Savvych (1722-1794). Ukrainian by birth, he was the earliest thinker in Russia who may appropriately be called a philosopher. He has been termed "the Russian Socrates." A poet and theologian as well as a philosopher, he knew Hebrew, Greek, Latin, and German, as well as Russian and Ukrainian. He travelled widely in Europe, spending most of his life as an itinerant teacher of morals. He wrote brilliant philosophical dialogues that show the influence of Plato, with a mystical coloring.

Socrates (ca. 470-399 B.C.E.). Greek philosopher who was the teacher of Plato. Socrates said that an oracle of the gods had pronounced him the wisest of all people, because he knew how little he knew. The Socratic method of teaching proceeds by question and answer as opposed to lecture or dogmatic assertion. When Socrates was elderly, the citizens of Athens condemned him to death, alleging that he denied the reality of the gods and corrupted the youth of Athens.

Solomon (11th-10th centuriesB.C.E.). King of Israel. Famed throughout the Orient for his wisdom. Traditionally considered the author of such books of the *Bible* as *The Song of Songs*.

Spencer, Herbert (1820-1903). English philosopher. Before Darwin published *The Origin of Species*, Spencer advanced the idea of evolution. As a sociologist, he applied this notion of evolution to social entities. He originally coined the phrase "survival of the fittest."

Strakhov, Fyodor Alekseevich (1861-1923). Russian author of philosophical writings whose views coincided with those of Tolstoy in many respects.

Sufi Writings. Documents of an Islamic movement known as Sufism, that believes that the individual will find salvation through personal union with Allah and emphasizes the need for asceticism in everyday life. The Sufis first arose in the eighth century C.E. Sometimes their views have differed considerably from the mainstream Islamic view; some, for example, taught that religious creeds are unimportant, that good and evil are unrealities, that there is no such thing as free will, and that ecstatic union with Allah is possible in this life. Much Sufi teaching and devotion is expressed in poetry of great emotional depth and intensity.

Talmud. A collection of rabbinical teachings compiled between the destruction of Jerusalem (70 C.E.) and the end of the fifth century. It is regarded as the highest legal authority in Judaism after the five original books of the Torah. It consists of interpretations of scripture, rules of hygiene and diet, legal decisions, and regulations for synagogue services. It also includes sermons, folklore, and legends, and sets out how faithful Jews should lead their lives both in family and in the world.

Tetskuko Nezagual Copotl. Aztec ruler who wrote his last will and testament in 1460 B.C.E.

Thomas a Kempis (1379-1471). Christian spiritual writer, active in the Netherlands. He wrote *Of the Imitation of Christ* (also known as *The Following of Christ*), a book which has been described as the most popular and influential book of the Christian world, and the greatest devotional book ever written. Its very simple and forcefully direct language reinforced its appeal; thousands of editions have been printed in more than fifty languages. It advocates a personal approach to spiritual life, based on introspection and mental focusing.

Thoreau, Henry David (1817-1862). American author who urged simple and honest approaches to life. He was a strong advocate of individual rights and was an opponent of social conformity. He was jailed briefly in the 1840s for refusing to pay a tax to support the Mexican War. His best known works are the book *Walden* and the essay *Civil Disobedience*.

Tucker, Benjamin Ricketson (1854-1939). American reformer and philosophical anarchist who felt that the state should be abolished and that individuals (or voluntary groups of individuals) should plan all activity. He vehemently opposed state control of social reform and felt individuals were capable of conducting their own lives. He opposed any violence in the realization of this individualism. He founded the journals *Radical Review* and *Liberty* and believed that monopoly and privileges should be abolished, and opportunity given to all along with the encouragement of competition.

Viveka-Chudamani (*The Crest-Jewel of Discrimination*). Classic Hindu spiritual text by the major spiritual master Shankara (ca. 686-718). With brutal frankness, it condemns this world of illusion and its apparent pleasures. It stresses the way of discrimination and advocates self-control and renunciation while urging us to see all creatures and objects in their true relation to the Absolute.

Vivekananda, Swami (1863-1902). Disciple of Sri Ramakrishna and dynamic founder of the Ramakrishna monastic order. Played an essential role in disseminating awareness of Vedanta and Hinduism in the West in the 1890s. He is best remembered for his pronouncement that all religions are true. For the first time, his writings presented to the western reader in clear and modern language the rationale for meditation and other spiritual exercises as fostered by Hinduism. He also advocated the practice of social service in a spirit of total commitment to the needs of the destitute and ailing.

Voice of Silence, The. Late 19th century spiritual classic, edited by Helena Petrovna Blavatsky.

Voltaire (1694-1778). French philosopher and writer, and a major figure of the Enlightenment. (The Enlightenment was an intellectual movement of the 17th and 18th centuries marked by a celebration of the powers of human reason, a keen interest in science, the promotion of religious toleration, and a desire to construct a government free of tyranny.) He wrote several tragedies, a comedy, poems, essays, stories and novellas, articles and pamphlets, and the *Treatise on Tolerance*. The most famous of his works is *Candide*. As militant social critic, he wrote numerous essays, pamphlets, and articles denouncing political abuses, corruption, war, the inequality of resources, mores of his day, undue literary reputations, and false religion and fanaticism. As a result of his endeavors and protests, he obtained reversals of unfair court decisions or condemnations.

Wilkins, George (1785-1865). English religious writer and preacher who was noted for his oratory skills and involvement with church restoration. In 1839, he resigned all his preferments in order to look after the spiritual needs of people.

Wolseley, Sir Charles (1630?-1714). English writer and politician. He was allied with King Charles I during the Civil War, then was a member of the "Little Parliament" organized by Cromwell. After he was pardoned by Charles II, he took to writing pamphlets mostly concerning church and faith issues.

Xenophon (ca. 430-ca. 355 B.C.E.) Disciple of Socrates, Greek historian, and soldier who served with Agesilaus (king of Sparta), fighting against his native Athens. He has been viewed as an idealist who worked within the limitations of his environment. He was a champion of aristocratic ideals, the virtues of politics, war, rural life, and the traditional family. He felt that one should pursue an education as far as possible. He wrote the *Cyropaedia*, a treatise on political and military organization and on moral reform, which paints a positive picture of the conqueror Cyrus the Elder.

Zarathustra or **Zoroaster**. The founder of Zoroastrianism, who is believed to have lived around 1500 B.C.E. in Persia. Zarathustra came from a family of priests, and at first lived a settled family life. Then, at age 13 he had a series of visions of God, on the basis of which he began to preach. Zarathustra's teachings conflicted with the polytheism of the old religion, since he stated that the only good God was Ahura Mazda and that he would judge each individual soul after death.

Zschokke, Johann-Heinrich (1771-1848). Swiss actor, then priest. He was the author of novels and short stories, and a spokesperson for liberal views.